ART NEEDLEWORK

and

EMBROIDERY

TRANSFERS

1870-1970

Molly G Proctor

ART NEEDLEWORK and EMBROIDERY TRANSFERS 1870-1970

By Molly G Proctor

Copyright © 2009 Molly G Proctor

ISBN 978-1-4452-0001-9

Published by Richard & Judith Proctor
28 Diprose Road, Corfe Mullen, Wimborne, Dorset, BH21 3QY, UK

Published through lulu.com

CONTENTS

Introduction	4
The Invention of the Hot-Iron Transfer	6
Victorian Patterns	13
Traced Needlework	22
Art Nouveau 1900-1920	34
Art Deco 1920-1939	47
Needle Etchings and Other Pictures	57
Occupational Therapy	71
The Crinoline Lady	84
Appendices	88
Briggs Needle Etchings available at various times between 1930—1960s	88
Regimental and Other Badges	94
Sources of Art Needlework Designs	95
Bibliography	96
Index	97

ACKNOWLEDGEMENTS

I would like to thank Mr D McMillan, General Manager of William Briggs, the Deighton family, and Mr TE Beckett, formerly of Fairistytch, for their help in tracing the history of their companies and especially the dozens of past employees and hundreds of other people who have given me invaluable information, most of it previously unrecorded.

    The Library, Manchester Metropolitan University and Platt Hall Museum of Costume, Manchester, were helpful to Miss Pat Yarwood who carried out research there for me in connection with William Briggs. The Imperial War Museum willingly gave me access to their collection of occupational therapy needlework. Many other museums and organisations, including the Embroider's Guild, sent a polite reply to my request for information but regretted they had very little or none.

    Very special thanks to Sally Carss who put my pencilled words into her computer to make an easily read printout. Also to my son Richard, and his wife, Judith, for their skill and willing help in preparing the manuscript and illustrations for publication.

    Finally, without the help of my late husband I would have been unable to write this book ..... thank you.

    Molly G Proctor 2009

INTRODUCTION

This is the first book to record some of the best embroideries made with the guidance of a hot-iron transfer and how they were manufactured.

"It is a big mistake, and one too often made, to conclude that anything popular is worthless," Matt Ridley *Daily Telegraph*, June 1998. Embroidery transfers were sold in their millions for more than a hundred years to satisfy the demands of ordinary people all over the world who enjoyed using them. They were essentially an early do-it-yourself craft product aimed at the domestic market. Mr A Deighton, of Deighton's, which manufactured patterns from 1870, wrote this simple explanation:

"A hot-iron embroidery transfer has the outline of a design printed on light-weight paper in heat-activated ink. The melting point of the ink is low enough for it to be transferred to fabrics using an ordinary domestic iron, then it is ready for subsequent embroidery in colours selected by the user."

By 1860 there were few ladies who did not embroider as a hobby, only the poor were prevented from embellishing their homes to add a personal touch of luxury to everyday objects.

As the country's wealth continued to expand and suburbs were built around every town, countless manuals were published to instruct the middle classes on the correct way to live up to their new status. Although the quality of furniture and furnishings varied according to their owner's income, there was a great similarity between them and the immediate impression was one of clutter — the lack of material objects was equated with lack of money and that would never do! Ladies' magazines included 'family reading', fashion and many suggestions for improving the home with needlework: either Berlin wool-work charts for canvas work or patterns printed in outline to be traced and transferred to fabric. Gradually the craze for Berlin wool-work diminished and, although by no means at an end, by the 1870s a new form of embroidery was beginning to take its place.

In 1872 the Royal School of Art Needlework (now the Royal School of Needlework) was opened in London, followed by many Schools of Art in the provinces where a new style of embroidery was taught: "'Art Needlework', a general term for all descriptions of needlework that spring from the application of a knowledge of design and colouring." *Dictionary of Needlework, Caulfield & Saward, 1882.* There was a re-awakening of interest in embroidery encouraged by William Morris and his contemporaries in the Arts and Crafts Movement, but their new ideas had little effect on families of modest means because it was too expensive — they continued to admire the old, familiar designs for many years to come.

The proliferation of popular designs was influenced by economics — the small fancy work shop, large departmental store or the magazine proprietor had to make a profit, so they trod the safest path and promoted goods that sold well. This has always made good business sense. New ideas took a very long time to reach the High Street.

To create a design and enhance it with needlework is exciting and satisfying but the few original embroideries that come on to the market are difficult to find; anything connected to a well-known artist or fashionable style can be very expensive and some experimental works do not appeal to everyone. The vast majority of women and some men found creating an original design too difficult to be a pleasure and very occasionally a respected name in embroidery actually admitted some workers did not possess the skill to do this but needed guidance from a prepared pattern. From mid-Victorian times there was an ever-increasing number of ladies with time and money to spend on fancy work, but not the skill to work unaided. What was needed were cheap patterns that were easy to use, and the invention of the hot-iron transfer did just that.

The number of transfers and embroideries created from them which have survived is absolutely enormous, but it must be said they are not all works of art. However, amongst them is a wonderful heritage of artistic and interesting needlework waiting to be discovered, much of it eminently collectable. Transfers were as popular between 1880-1960 as Berlin wool-work had been during Victoria's reign and both were dismissed by the art world as a waste of time. As Berlin wool compliments Victorian Furnishings, Art Needlework designs have their place later.

Very few museums have collected interesting examples of transfers or embroideries worked from them because they do not consider them to be an important part of the history of needlework, although they gave so much pleasure to ordinary folk. I have purposely omitted poor examples and tried to show the best aspects of the craft — the work of talented designers and the embroideries of gifted people who needed a little bit of help from a hot-iron transfer.

It is not possible to include all the various types of needlework which used transfers, because the range is almost unlimited. Whatever takes your fancy, there are almost certainly embroideries to be found from canvas work to cross stitch, broderie anglaise to appliqué, felt work, bead work and so on. It is the same with particular subjects. There are cartoon characters such as 'Felix the Cat' or 'Pip, Squeak and Wilfred', Dutch scenes, ethnic designs from around the world, nursery rhymes, animals, birds, butterflies and, of course, probably every flower in the nurseryman's catalogue….

THE INVENTION OF THE HOT-IRON TRANSFER

The two most important names in the history of the hot-iron transfer are William Briggs of Manchester and William Deighton of London. During the late 1860s it is probable both men were experimenting to find a process whereby an embroidery pattern could easily be transferred from paper to fabric in the home; each discovered a solution, but by a different method.

Because Briggs applied for a patent in 1874 he has been given credit for the invention, but this is only partly true. His original method was to apply a special ink to a stamping block or cylinder roller and print a design on to thin paper. He used this exclusively for four or five years.

Deighton's invention needed a perforating machine which offered a more versatile process, but he did not patent the idea in spite of selling his transfers in London from 1870. By 1880 Briggs had adopted a perforating machine for elaborate designs and eventually one was used by all manufacturers for all transfers.

From the early years the two men were in dispute over claims to the invention, which resulted in a protracted court case and long-term rivalry between the companies. Unfortunately, when Briggs was absorbed into the Coats Group, all their records were destroyed and it is difficult to find reliable information; Deighton's early archives were also lost. The whole truth may never be discovered but some facts are known.

In the 1860s William Deighton was a talented designer in the textile trade. It is believed he evolved an idea for the home market to print designs for embroidery on to fabric and discussed this with his father, a surgeon and apothecary of Bethnal Green, London. The result was the development of a heat-activated ink, but it was so viscous with waxes and resins that no conventional printing process was possible. As the ink had to be applied in a layer sufficiently thick to allow the colour to transfer from the paper to the fabric, it took several hours to harden and to dry enough to be handled. Deighton adapted the centuries-old method of prick and pounce whereby a design is drawn on paper and small holes pricked along every line. The paper is placed over the fabric and powder rubbed through the holes; this produces a line of dots underneath which can be fixed permanently with paint. He made a machine known as a perforator to make the pin holes (*fig 1*). One owned by the

1. Deighton's original perforator

present Deighton family may be the original model and I am indebted to my husband for the following description of it:

"The perforating machine was positioned behind the work surface and consisted of a treadle-operated fly wheel, housed in a wooden frame, which drove a reciprocating needle (i.e. one that falls and rises like a sewing machine) by means of a series of pulleys. The hand-held needle mechanism was well-balanced and could easily be moved horizontally over a 30 cm square area of parchment paper. The needle was secured by means of a chuck, and an adjustable stop assisted its clean withdrawal and also controlled the depth of penetration" (*fig 2*).

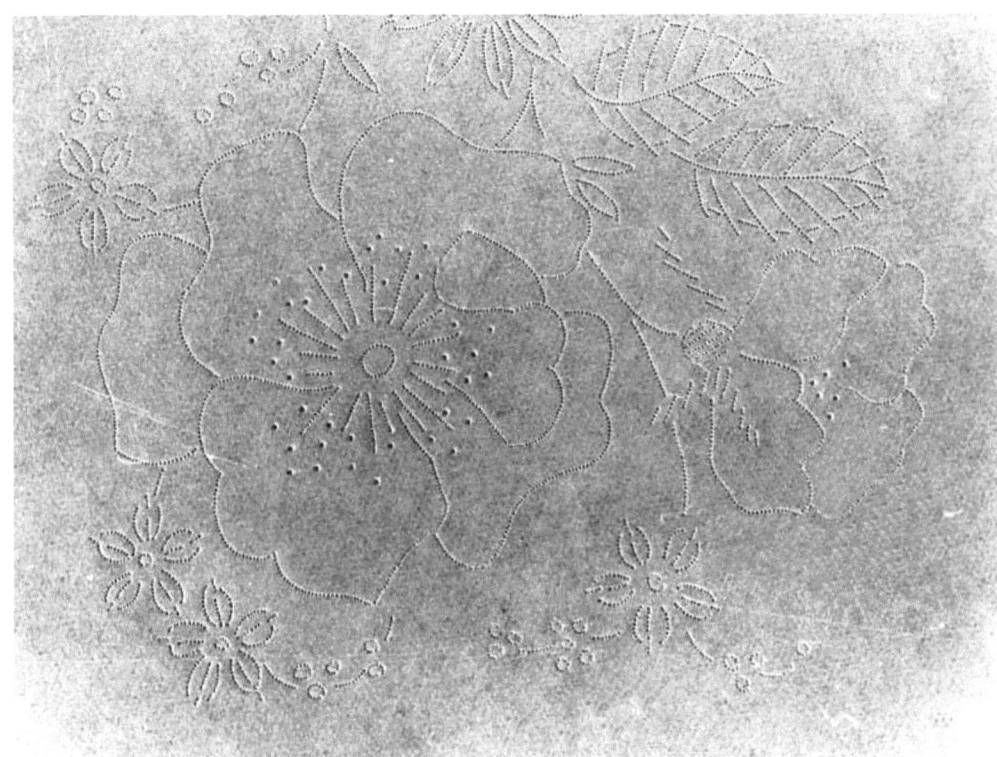

2. Perforated design on stout paper, Briggs 1930s

The following description of the early manufacture of transfers draws on scant information from Deighton's and Briggs.

The workroom had a large library of illustrated books, predominately plant life including seedsmen's catalogues. An idea was sketched in charcoal or pencil and, if approved by the head designer, was worked into a suitable pattern and tinted with crayons (*fig 3*). The final drawing was built up using several layers of very thin paper; for example, an individual flower on the first sheet, buds and leaves on the next and finally a ribbon. A master on translucent paper was created by tracing the original design and this was then placed over three or four heavy sheets of paper. A skilled operator pricked along the outlines on the master using the perforator and created three or four identical stencils, each of which could be used several times. Next, the perforated stencil was laid in position over one sheet of white tissue-type paper and held in position with a heavy tailor's iron. The special mixture of 'ink' was applied to the surface of the stencil and forced through the pin holes using a fabric pad. The transfers were hung on giant horizontal frames to dry overnight — it is said William Deighton hung his early efforts over the banisters.

3. Design on tracing, paper hand-coloured with crayons, Briggs 1930s

By examining most pre-1950 transfers, the apparently continuous lines are actually a series of minute dots. Eventually, the process for producing transfers was mechanised and a special ink, imported from the USA, allowed the use of a printing press.

The Deighton family believe that having devised a method of printing the transfers William was ready to test his ability as a salesman, so he put some into a wicker skip and walked to the most likely shops in London. The firm of Deighton Brothers Ltd always gave 1870 as the year they first sold hot-iron transfers, from information in a legal document (to be discussed later) - it was certainly before William Briggs' patent was sealed on 29 June 1875.

William Deighton's enterprise was very successful, sales grew and the quantities required became larger than could be handled at home. He purchased another house, with a large workshop in the garden, situated in Mayola Road, Clapton, London, (these premises were previously owned by William Booth, founder of the Salvation Army which had its Citadel nearby). Deighton Brothers used this building until about 1960 when they moved to Bristol and later to Barnstable, Devon. At one time they also had factories in Dublin and Belfast.

In 1840 in the village of Blackely, now a suburb of Manchester, James Briggs established himself as a manufacturer of floor lubricants, and at one time his son, William, traded as a drapery and fancy goods merchant, probably from the same building. It is not known when William moved but in 1874 he was in business at 3 Marsden Square, Manchester from where, on 29 December of that year, John Briggs, engraver to calico printers, Richard Hudson, designer, and Henry Grimshaw, hatter, applied to the

4. Sample of appliqué on black satin, made in Briggs' workroom

Commissioners of Patents with a Provisional Specification for the invention of: *Improvements in Ornamenting and Transferring Patterns to Fabric*.

> '..... we hereby declare the nature of our Invention and what manner the same is to be performed......
> Our Invention consists in transferring the pattern to the fabric to be ornamented or embroidered by printing the paper pattern from a surface block or otherwise as usual with the design to be produced in a bituminous substance or varnish and transferring the said pattern to the fabric when required by the application of heat to the back of the paper on which the pattern has been printed thereby causing the bitumen or varnish to adhere to the fabric to be ornamented or embroidered.
> ..... we make no claim to any process or apparatus for printing the pattern by blocks or cylinders our Invention is printing the said patterns on pattern paper and transferring them to fabric by heat.'

Doubtless William Briggs was selling hot-iron transfers from his shop and elsewhere before the patent was sealed. He prospered and by 1889 had moved to larger premises in Cannon Street, Manchester. This was later demolished and in 1914 a new ferro-concrete building erected on the site. In 1963 the company moved to an old mill in Bolton and re-located during the 1990s to an industrial estate in nearby Halliwell.

An early example of Briggs Transferring Papers is a box containing several six-yard strips of scalloped edgings. As there is no name on the wrappers, we know they were made before 1877 (*Fig 5a*). Between 1877 and 1881 wrappers were printed with William Briggs Company and the family arms. The following year Briggs became a Registered Company and in 1895 a Limited Company.

The earliest transfers have BRIGGS and a number (indicating the number of the design) stamped by hand in indelible mauve ink at one end of each paper, and are wrapped in a narrow blue band with these instructions:

> 'To Transfer the Design use a HOT IRON (Medium Heat). For Flannel, Serge etc. Iron must be HOT (Full Laundry Heat)'

A yellow label is tucked under each band:

> 'Use a HOT IRON (Medium Heat). For Serge Flannel or very Fluffy Materials Iron to be full laundry heat. Smooth material first with Iron. For SILK, WHITE LINEN and COTTON Iron to be warm only or the mark will be too strong. (Use a yellow transfer)
> Place the material on a level and hard surface. Press the Iron down hard and quickly for one second, not more. Don't glide over. Repeat this until the whole pattern is transferred and do not iron over the same place twice unless the paper sticks.

If after ironing the pattern should be slightly indistinct, scratch lightly with the fingernail

To erase the pattern use Benzene'

Another box of scalloped edgings with the family arms on the wrapper (*Fig 5b*) (after 1877) has this slogan on the box lid:

'BRIGGS are the SOLE inventors of the process of transferring patterns by heat.'

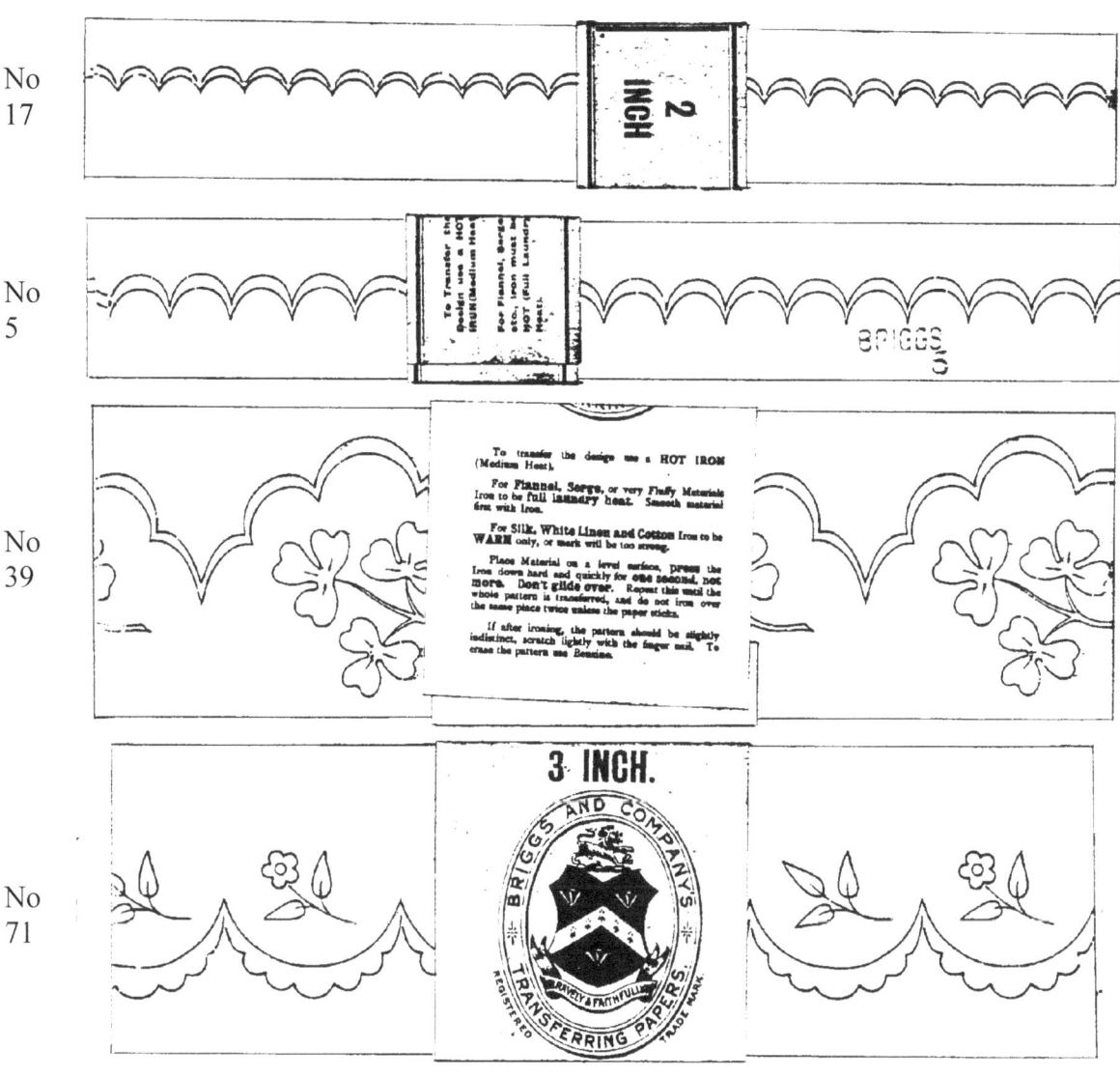

5a. Transfers number 17 and 5 manufactured before 1877
5b. Number 39 and 71 between 1877 and 1881, Briggs

William Deighton knew this was untrue and must have intimated this to William Briggs which initiated a protracted legal battle. Some singed legal documents concerning the case survived a bonfire at Deighton's premises in the mid-1970s at the time they were taken over by William Briggs & Co Ltd. They are in the possession of the Deighton family.

On 17 December 1880 William Briggs and his partner, the Reverend Christopher Cronshaw of Bolton, Lancashire, brought an action against William Deighton for alleged infringement of their patent. In his defence Deighton testified the invention was not new at the time the patent was granted and although the court found in favour of Briggs there must have been some truth in the defendant's plea as litigation continued. The following year Briggs and Deighton agreed to a compromise and signed a Legal Agreement on 20 December 1881. It appears they agreed to share production under the letters patent, Briggs to supply Deighton with paper transfers at 25% below market price, and Deighton to reciprocate and submit all his stock of transfers which did infringe copyright to Briggs to be stamped 'Briggs Patent', for which Briggs would waive any costs or damages against him. Finally, and very important to subsequent events, Briggs would employ Deighton as a designer at £100 per annum, payable quarterly, and pay him additional sums for all designs accepted. Deighton kept his side of the Agreement but Briggs did not.

On 20 February 1883, William Deighton issued a writ in the High Court against Briggs & Co as they had only paid him one quarterly payment of £25 then refused to pay or stamp any more of Deighton's transfers which rendered them unsaleable. Their most damaging action was, however, a circular letter sent to all Deighton's customers:

> 'High Court of Justice Chancery Division
> As solicitors for Briggs & Co ..... we give you notice that of 17 December 1881 the above court granted an injunction in favour of the plaintiff restraining the defendants during the continuance of the plaintiff's letters patent ..... from using or selling any patterns for the purpose of transfer to fabrics ..... that is to say by the application of heat ..... and we give you further notice that legal proceedings will be commenced against any other person who may infringe the said letters patent.'

A rider, signed 23 April 1883, was added:

> 'Messrs Briggs & Co undertake not to issue any more circulars or to make any statement to the detriment of the plaintiff (William Deighton) in respect of patterns or goods stamped by the defendant (Briggs & Co) until after the trial of this action.'

All subsequent documents relating to the action have probably been lost or destroyed, at least so far no record has been found, but the Deighton family believe they won the case. The Briggs catalogue, 1882, clearly shows the use of a perforator. Did Briggs use the Deighton invention? Were some of the designs drawn by William Deighton? Both seem probable. Both firms remained in business.

VICTORIAN PATTERNS

Before 1882 Briggs published *Designs for all Kinds of Embroidery* but a copy has not been discovered.

In 1882 or 1883 *Briggs & Co Patent Transferring Papers* was issued (revised and enlarged a few years later), a hardback book with about five hundred designs. The catalogue was probably distributed free by Briggs to their agents or could be borrowed from the London printer for a few pence per week.

The frontispiece described transfers as:

> 'Now universally known and acknowledged to be the most perfect, simple and expeditious manner of tracing designs for embroidery. One of the great recommendations of these Transferring Papers is that they enable ladies to trace their own materials, this being much less expensive than purchasing ready-traced articles. New designs are frequently being issued.'

Many contemporary writers decided to ignore transfers, the comprehensive two-volume *Dictionary of Needlework*, Caulfield & Saward, also published in 1882, did not mention them.

The catalogue was in sections starting with borders varying in width up to eight inches (20 cm)[1]. These were followed by sprays (*fig* 6) and groups of flowers, doilies, cushions, footstools, cosies, chair seats, antimacassars, table or piano corners, aprons or pinafores, slippers and pillow shams, finally, five ecclesiastical motifs.

Over 90% of the designs were floral but the over-blown cabbage roses, cactus, auriculas and other vivid blossoms which had adorned Berlin wool-work on canvas were replaced by simple plants from the English countryside (*fig* 7) and newly-planted gardens — wild roses, daisies, cornflowers or forget-me-nots.

Every design had a number and, it may be significant for dating, the lowest for scalloped edgings, braiding designs and alphabets.

'..... as braiding is now more fashionable than ever it is no slight thing to be able to obtain your design and tracing apparatus in one.' *Sylvia's Home Journal, 1882.*

6. *Briggs & Co's Patent Transferring Papers 1882/3*

1. All measurements are as given in the contemporary source, i.e. inches, with approximate equivalent metric size in brackets

Briggs transfers for braiding were available in various widths and the designs could be arranged to form separate ornaments or borders. Braids were considered particularly suitable for ladies' dresses and mantles (figs 8, 9, 10). They were also popular for various small knickknacks such as blotters, watch pockets and albums, and especially for gentlemen's smoking caps, waistcoats and slippers (*Fig* 11).

Unfortunately, gentlemen did not always appreciate decorative items of clothing and in

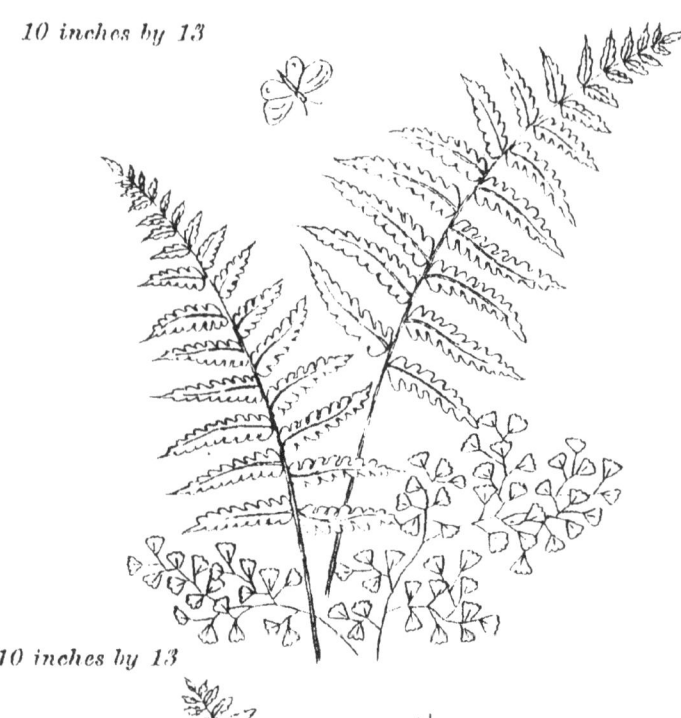

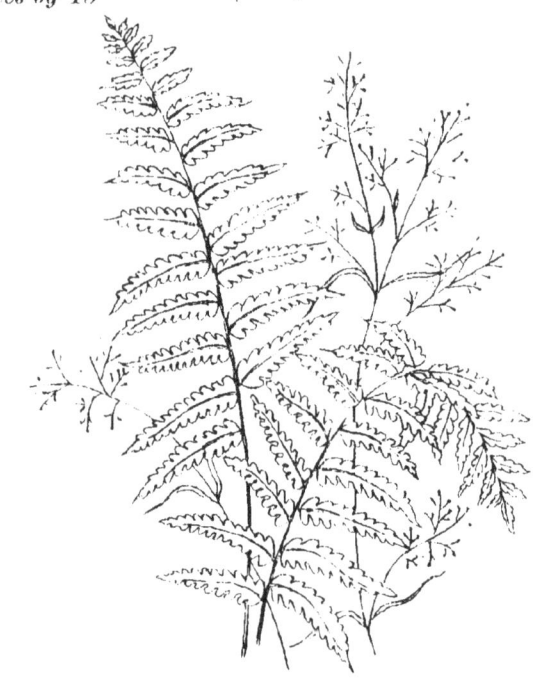

8 *Braiding Transfer Briggs & Co's Patent Transferring Paper* 1882/3, Design 4 inches by 8

7. *Briggs & Co's Patent Transferring Papers* 1882/3

9: *Braiding Transfer Briggs & Co's Patent Transferring Papers* 1882/3

10: *Braiding Transfer Briggs & Co's Patent Transferring Paper* 1882/3, Design 5½ inches by 5

11: *Briggs & Co's Patent Transferring Papers* 1882/3

1889, the American magazine *Needlecraft* offered some useful advice: 'Suitable gifts for a lady to present to a gentleman must be useful, ornamental and easily made by deft fingers moving to the music of happy thoughts.' The Briggs braiding designs for slippers were restrained, but others showing a hunting scene, a kangaroo and smoking artefacts for crewel work were anything but! Transfers for smoking caps and slippers were still manufactured in the 1930s.

Many Victorian personal and household linens were marked with an initial or monogram and although an alphabet in cross stitch was easy to sew, anything more decorative required some guidance. Briggs manufactured transfers of simple letters from the earliest days and soon added more decorative designs. The 1882 catalogue included the alphabet (no 'Q' or 'X') in small, medium or large Old English, Italic or Floral, the later edition had eleven styles in six sizes, ½ to 3½ inches (1-9 cm), and several alphabets intended for broderie anglaise. After 1895 Briggs' initials were sold in small booklets with a coloured cover to indicate the typeface and were kept in production indefinitely. Several other companies produced similar items.

There is a wealth of household linen offered for sale decorated with initials and other motifs embroidered in white. The linen or fine cotton is of superb quality: do not buy damaged pieces.

At a glance, several pages of designs look suitable for ordinary cross-stitch but they were intended for Russian embroidery, a Berlin wool-work novelty stitched on felt or other plain fabric. The *Dictionary of Needlework* explained the tedious method: 'Coarse canvas is placed over suitable fabric and the embroidery worked through both. When complete the canvas threads are withdrawn one at a time.' On a completed piece of work it is difficult to identify the traditional method from a transferred design worked straight on to the felt.

12. Birds c1880 with hand-written lettering, Briggs

Whoever drew the pictures of birds (*fig 12*) and children for the 1882 catalogue was not very good at it. Unfortunately, many artists were producing work totally unsuitable for the medium of embroidery, even Kate Greenaway's (1846-1901) copyright 'Village Scenes' (published by Briggs & Co as a booklet catalogue) were no better. *Peterson's Magazine*, an American publication, commented: '..... in general public taste left much to be desired', but not everyone thought the same. *Myra's Journal of Dress and Fashion*, a Weldon's publication, considered: '..... these children are entirely superseding the storks of which we have had more than enough and are certainly more amusing than those meaningless birds', although several issues of *Weldon's Ladies' Journal* included large transfers of storks in Japanese scenes intended for portières and screens. In the revised edition of the Briggs catalogue all the children were omitted, but there were still plenty of birds and butterflies of doubtful merit.

From 1840 there had been much building work and restoration of Anglican and Roman Catholic churches. The first public condemnation of Berlin wool-work had come from the Church and following this architects and suitable artists were commissioned to help restore the level of ecclesiastical embroidery. Briggs and Deighton's produced transfers with designs suitable for use in churches, many kept in production indefinitely and some to the present day (attributed to Deighton's but manufactured by Briggs since 1977). In addition to typical Gothic designs, Deighton's introduced a large range of attractive Celtic patterns which proved to be best sellers in spite of the very complicated designs, a large number of which were still available in 2008 by mail order from Copelands, Northern Ireland, makers of fine linens for the church and home market.

Myra's Journal of Dress and Fashion and *The Young Ladies' Journal* liked Briggs ecclesiastical designs: '..... they are a welcome change from the usual sprays and wreaths of flowers so much worked in the last few years. ..... some will serve admirably for valences for mantelpieces, curtains and tablecloth borders for use in rooms furnished in a rather severe style'.

It is unlikely Briggs continued to produce expensive comprehensive catalogues after they issued a range of specialist booklets at a penny each. An advertisement from the 1890s listed: Floral designs, Artistic and conventional designs, Ribbon work, Cross stitch, Braiding designs, Ecclesiastical designs and one with designs for chip carving in wood.

Weldon's was a very successful publisher with a head office in Southampton Street, near The Strand in London. About 1885 they issued the first of their popular series of *Practical Needlework*, but for a few years no transfers were available and the full-sized drawings had to be traced. It was not long, however, before Weldon's and Briggs had a working partnership and subsequently they produced all the transfers attributed to the publisher. Possibly the first mention of the connection between the two companies was in *Weldon's Practical Needlework No 19, Smocking*. The craft had been revived for ornamenting ladies' and children's clothing — tea gowns, bodices, underlinen and even a bathing suit made of serge or flannel. The booklet, dating from the early? 1890s, suggested several methods to create even gathers and 'Quite lately Mr Briggs has issued sheets of transfer papers with small dots at regular intervals; the sheets only require ironing on the material in the same manner as Briggs well-known designs for crewel work.' Smocking dots were not in the 1882 catalogue but probably were introduced shortly afterwards.

In 1889 the Butterick Publishing Co, New York, produced the hardback book *Needlecraft Artistic and Practical*, a collection of articles taken from their magazine *The Delineator*. It included instructions for making one's own 'stampings' to transfer a pattern on to cloth:

> 'Lay transparent parchment paper over the design to be transferred and with a lead pencil reproduce all the lines. With a tracing wheel follow these outlines. Lay perforated paper upon the material and rub over the lines with a good stamping powder, blue or white. Remove stamping paper, lay a piece of tissue paper over the goods and pass a warm iron slowly over it. The design will be accurately reproduced.'

Ingalls of Massachusetts, a maker of stamping powder, advertised a catalogue of stamping patterns for alphabets and floral designs suitable for table covers, tidies, sofa pillows, aprons, etc. The roses, ferns, daisies, fuchsia, clover, nasturtiums, morning glory, lily of the valley, forget-me-not, pansy and poppy were Briggs' designs. Ingalls was a 'Special Mail Agent' for Briggs and imported the patterns for American consumers. Ingalls published a copy of the Briggs Transferring catalogue for its customers.

No reference at this time to a similar product in Britain has been found but this was published in *Manufacturers' Practical Recipes*, 1929:

24 lbs lamp black
7 lbs finely powdered resin
Process — well mix

During the 1930s and 1940s *Weldon's Encyclopaedia of Needlework* (reprinted several times) suggested the use of transfer ink to trace the outlines of a design which when dry could be transferred to the material in the usual way. An often repeated idea in inexpensive books of the same period used a mixture of caster sugar and Reckett's Washing Blue (a powder added to rinsing water to improve the colour of whites) applied to an old transfer to make it re-useable. Today there are several products available to transfer a design on to fabric.

During the nineteenth century it is known Briggs exported transfers throughout the British Empire and the USA. Deighton's also supplied this market but no records have been discovered. The March 1889 American edition of the *Young Ladies' Journal* carried a very small William Briggs advertisement for an Art Needlework competition for amateurs and professionals. A few years later Art Needlework had become very popular in the USA and many exhibitions took place.

Without doubt transfers had become popular with all classes of society, except the self-appointed arbiters of 'good taste' who scoffed at the amateur and her embroidery: 'Their aim and object is to elicit admiration from all beholders', *The Gentlewoman's Book of Art*

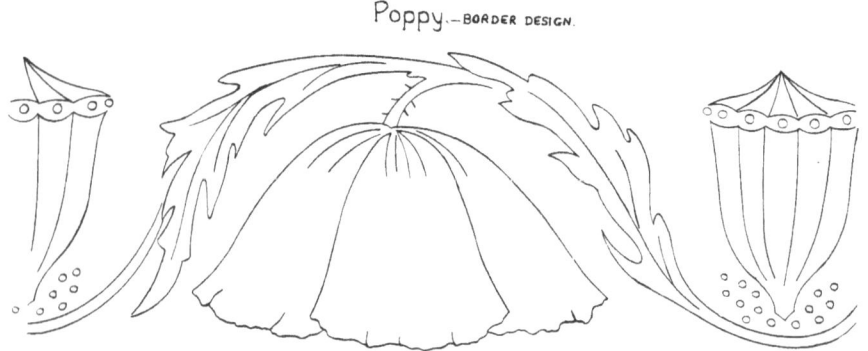

13. Briggs *Blanche Fitzmaurice Portfolio of Artistic Needlework* c 1890
All Saints Library Manchester Metropolitan University

Needlework, 1892. But widespread criticism had little effect and a few years later W G Paulson Townsend, a respected design master at the Royal School of Art Needlework admitted in *Embroidery or the Craft of the Needle* that comparatively few embroideresses designed their own patterns.

For about twenty years Briggs had used artists who were competent to produce run-of-the-mill patterns, but no more. Sometime during the 1890s the large *Blanche Fitzmaurice Portfolio of Artistic Needlework* (25 x 38 cm) was published. This contained a collection of designs by several artists of varied skills and among the patterns were some unexpected and extraordinary transfers (*fig 13*).

Probably the most amazing section had designs for enormous pictures suitable for portières (large door curtains, fashionable in Britain and the USA) bedspreads and window curtains; the largest, 8 x 5 feet (2.44 x 1.52 m) required ten transfers. Several of the massive designs had an Egyptian theme (*fig 14*), a popular subject after the opening of the Suez canal in 1869 and the later invasion of Egypt by the British army. There was a further upsurge of interest in 1922 with the discovery of Tutankhamen's tomb

14. Briggs *Blanche Fitzmaurice Portfolio of Artistic Needlework* circa 1890
Very large 8 feet x 5 feet (2.44 x 1.52m)
All Saints Library, Manchester Metropolitan University

and, by an unexpected co-incidence this happened in the very month that *Harmsworth's Fashions for All* featured 'Suitable Egyptian Designs'. All Briggs' patterns were packed with a busy jumble of motifs with few or no suggestions for colour or stitches — 'Admirably adapted to appliquéd velveteen on felt', or 'May be done in outline stitch'. Outline (stem) stitch, often in mono-colour, was chosen by many professional embroiderers for the large hangings created by well known artists, e.g. Edward Burne-Jones.

Huge, popular exhibitions which displayed arts from around the world influenced design. Japan was well represented in the Portfolio, for example *Leaping Fish* (*fig 15*), was probably inspired by a piece of porcelain and *Waves and Fishes* by a print but unfortunately, the latter had been drawn by more than one person and some details were crude. This was not uncommon, *Night Season* had a beautiful pine tree and toadstools ruined by flying bats and *The Swan*, glided past a fanciful tree, with the beak and talons of an eagle!

It would be very interesting to know the names of the artists who designed transfers. They are elusive, but it is quite wrong to dismiss all designers of transfer patterns as incompetent amateurs. Certainly by 1920, and probably earlier, most had been trained at art schools and some well-respected and successful artists and teachers of embroidery are known to have designed commercial transfers, especially for high quality journals. Constance Brown, 1881-1978, studied at the Royal College of Art and produced work for *The Embroideress*. *Shirly* (*sic*), one of the designs in the Fitzmaurice Portfolio, could easily be the work of Arthur Mackmurdo who founded the Century Guild and promoted Art Nouveau in the 1880s and 1890s, but unfortunately, *Shirly's* sinuous, flame-like plant shapes probably originated as a woodcut and the artist did not appreciate the limitations of embroidery. Some transfers included a motto or a couple of lines of poetry.

If the designers of commercial transfers had been acknowledged, would this have altered the opinions of the art critics?

15: Briggs *Blanche Fitzmaurice Portfolio of Artistic Needlework* circa 1890
All Saints Library, Manchester Metropolitan University

Mention must be made of one type of decoration found at this period that was rarely successful nor socially acceptable, that of using imitation jewels and beetle wings: '... unless you have displayed very good taste the work will have a common look which I am sure will not appeal to you.' *Art Needlework*, Mrs Townsend.

It is difficult to confirm or deny claims by Briggs and Deighton about particular shops that sold their transferring papers during the nineteenth century. Although Harrods' catalogue 1895 gave Briggs as the maker, the very large catalogue of the drapery wholesaler, Jeremiah Rotherham, did not name the manufacturer for their transfers suitable for appliqué, alphabets, chenille work, mantle borders, curtains, cushions, antimacassars, bed pockets, chair seats, handkerchiefs, 'monograms or coronets for saddle cloths for people who keep carriages and designs for the ornamental towel so frequently suspended in front of the useful towel in the bedroom'. Many wholesalers and retailers sold goods under their own name, but it is unlikely that they manufactured transfers or any of their other lines.

Mr William Briggs considered teaching and helping his customers to be important but the firm never traded direct with the public. In spite of this Mr Briggs realised that business would improve if he had a retail outlet in Manchester, and Mrs Bidder, Art Needlework Specialist, St Anne's Passage, was the answer. The shop was quite close to Cannon Street and stocked the full range of Briggs' merchandise, offered free advice and a postal service. Mrs Bidder kept her shop open far longer than her allotted life span and did not close until the 1960s when Briggs moved from Manchester. In spite of what customers believed, Mrs Bidder was not called 'Penelope' (registered in 1886 for various items sold by Briggs) — Neither Penelope or Mrs Bidder ever existed.

In 1896 Briggs published their first of many instruction booklets, *The First Book of Hows — Embroidery Stitches*, then *First Lessons* to teach basic stitches to school children. Both were issued under the name of 'The Manchester School of Needlework, Cannon Street'; this was not an educational establishment but the address of Briggs' factory and wholesale warehouse.

16: Above and left: *Briggs & Co's Patent Transferring Papers* 1882/3

TRACED NEEDLEWORK

Customers bought traced needlework as household linens, novelties and some items of clothing. It was an alternative to using a transfer at home, the design having been stamped on to the article at the factory by the manufacturer (*fig 17*). An advertisement by Wakefield Bros, Manchester Warehousemen and Wholesale Cash Drapers, was published frequently in *Weldon's Practical Journal* during the 1880s and 1890s: 'Traced felt and plush needlework in all the newest Art Shades — biscuit, mushroom, drab, slate, terracotta, peacock, olive and bronze. Endless Needlework Novelties in many new tracings ...'

17. Traced shelf hanging (one of a set of three) worked on plush with chenille thread. Manufacturer unknown.

Although traced linens were always more expensive than a paper transfer they were simpler to use and very popular. Briggs considered the introduction of 'Penelope' traced linens to be one of the main contributions to the company's success. To begin with instructions for working were fairly basic with, perhaps, appropriate numbers for the coloured threads, but once they were sold in packets, each included a coloured photograph, instructions for every stitch and sometimes actual skeins of stranded cotton or silks.

Briggs claimed to have originated the needlepack for servicemen in the late 1930s, but this was untrue. For example, in 1923 an *Art Needle Krafts* catalogue, published in New

York, included a large range of packs for household linens, children's wear and lingerie, and in January 1930 *The Needlewoman* promoted a similar idea which proved to be a successful venture.

Before the introduction of detailed instructions some traced needlework was sold 'commenced'. This implied, in addition to the transfer stamped on the fabric, a small section of the embroidery had been completed before sale to indicate the type of stitches and colours to use. Small shops, large stores, several ecclesiastical suppliers and even the Royal School of Art Needlework employed women for this work. Some retailers also offered to complete partly-worked items for a small charge.

18. 'Conventional Floral Spray' *Embroidery* August 1908 sold as commenced or plain traced. Deightons.

19. Sideboard cloth on coloured linen *Embroidery* August 1908 sold as commenced or plain traced. Deightons.

One magazine which offered plain traced or commenced work was *Embroidery*, 1908-9, (not connected with the publication of the same name published later by the Embroiderers' Guild). This journal was promoted by James Pearsall, the manufacturer of silk threads, and edited by Mrs Archibald (Grace) Christie, 1872-1938, a prolific writer on embroidery. The designs were simple and artistic and the magazine was printed to a very high standard intended for educated readers. Unfortunately, it was not successful. One edition had a floral spray in black, blue, gold and greens for a large hanging (*fig 18*), a conventional design of roses for a sideboard cloth (*fig 19*), a tea cosy and a pretty yoke for a child's dress (*fig 20*).

23

The price for commenced pieces was treble the amount for plain traced, but included all the silks. It is probable the transfers were made by Deighton's. In 1914 Pearsall and Mrs Christie tried again with *Needle and Thread*, a similar journal of high quality with excellent illustrations, but this closed after six editions because of the outbreak of the First World War.

Traced linens were made by the majority of transfer manufacturers and some specialist firms, but once embroidered it is almost impossible to distinguish the use of an iron-on transfer from a traced linen. Pre-1970 transfer ink always disappeared during washing, modern ink may not. It is also equally difficult to know if the name on a wrapper was the manufacturer or the distributor.

All early manufacturers who specialised in Art Needlework have ceased trading or been absorbed into other companies and their records lost or destroyed. Even Companies House, a government department working with the Public Record Office, have not kept early information about Deighton's or Briggs — once the largest manufacturers of these items in the world — but fortunately with determination and a lot of luck the past can sometimes yield very interesting information, even without official archives.

20. Yoke and band for a child's dress Worked on unbleached linen. *Embroidery* August 1908 sold as commenced or plain traced. Deightons.

Thomas Fuller Beckett, born 1881, began work as a representative for James Pearsall, the silk thread manufacturer. In 1919, with financial help from close friends, he launched the company T F Beckett & Co (Fairistytch) Ltd, Glasgow. Fairistytch became one of the leading manufacturers of high-quality traced linens and in 1948 received royal patronage. Many people considered their floral designs were among the best ever produced for the home market or abroad. The quality of stitchery and choice of colours used in samples made for shop display and catalogue illustrations was outstanding (*figs 21, 22*). There can be few embroideries guided by a transferred design that were more perfect. Some pieces were worked by demonstrators in stores or at exhibitions, a few were embroidered locally by Mr Beckett's two sisters, but the majority were posted to Madeira to be stitched by hand to an exacting standard. The island of Madeira is the centre of a well-known embroidery industry

21. Traced linen Fairistych 1930, worked in Madeira for display item. Contemporary 'Sunderland' china

and the women are experts in all types of needlework, especially the fine delicate white embroidery known as Madeira work. All the embroidery is executed to perfection with incredible speed and has always been produced for export on a large commercial scale.

Although the formula for 'ink' or 'paint' used by Briggs and Deighton's is not known there is a record from the paint manufacturer who supplied Beckett. It was made by Hamilton's, near Glasgow, and, surprisingly, when the business was taken over their records survived. This order was invoiced to T F Beckett, dated December 1927:

    Prussian blue powder
    White powder ATM Timonex Red
      (trade name for antimony oxide, a white pigment)
    Black powder carbon black
    White lithophane
      (zinc sulphide, an extender-type white pigment)

22: Traced linen 'Mixed Flowers' Fairistych 1930s worked in Madeira for catalogue photograph. Note the decorative hem.

An employee of Briggs described how a design was put on to fabric in about 1925:

"After the perforator had worked through four sheets of paper following the design on the wrong side, one sheet was placed on the material and a mixture of dry powder pigment and gum arabic rubbed through the perforations using a felt pad and then fixed with a hot iron. Each perforation could be used two or three times before it needed to be replaced."

Sometime after 1946 Fairistytch altered the formula for the transfer ink and added cellulose varnish containing benzene or toluene and white spirit which produced a blue paste that dried more quickly. An employee described her work:

23: Traced linen Briggs 1951, worked by the author. Contemporary Susie Cooper china.

"I started at less than £2 a week but I enjoyed working for them. I started as an ironer and became a tracer. The item to be traced was placed on a table and two flat irons used to hold the perforated design down on the linen. Then a large pad was soaked in oil and dipped into a tin of blue paste which was rubbed over the perforations followed by another larger rubber which brought the pattern on to the item. It was a messy job."

Beckett's first premises at 16 St Enoch Square, Glasgow, had a workroom on the top floor and a small office and showroom in the flat below. A woman who began work as an ironer in the 1920s at ten shillings (50p) a week described the workroom:

"In winter it was freezing cold with a glass roof. The basins of water and sponges which we used for dampening the material would be a solid block of ice when starting work at 8am. Quite the reverse in summer with the sun streaming through the glass. The two designers were also the perforators and embroidered sample pieces. When I started work there was one machinist and four tracers. When we moved to larger premises in Renfrew Street I was now a cutter, all cut by the thread and singly because the tracers required a straight line when putting the designs on. We were all known as Fairies!"

The two women designers specialised in flowers remained with Fairistytch until it closed. (Additional artists employed later to introduce 'modern' styles were not so successful.) It may surprise critics of the transfer that although both these designers trained at the Glasgow School of Art at a time when it was at the forefront of making needlework an art in a new and original style, they created designs to imitate nature. If any school of art trained designers for the commercial world, the artists had to produce a saleable product. They had to draw what the market demanded (via trade feed-back from established retailers). The market demanded pretty flowers.

Fairistytch artists rarely drew from memory or copied illustrations. They found inspiration from local observations. They travelled in the Scottish Highlands where specimens were sketched and one or two blossoms picked to make accurate drawings later. This was not an original idea, for example the City of London Trade School also encouraged their 14-18 year old students to make a close study of plants while on rambles, a popular pastime in an era of cheap travel by bus or train to the countryside. The best selling Fairistytch flowers were lucky heather and the Scottish thistle, but many garden flowers featured on their linens, even with an occasional hint of Art Deco — a bold step for this company.

All manufacturers of traced linens were at the peak of production during the 1930s. Fairistytch employed over a hundred workers and had more than a thousand retail outlets in the United Kingdom and abroad especially Australia, New Zealand and South Africa. Deighton's and Briggs were also exporting and the former offered designs with flowers indigenous to particular countries. Large stores had regular promotions with demonstrations of Fairistytch linens, even at Kendal Milne, Manchester, a stone's throw from Briggs' premises! They supplied many top quality stores with exclusive designs, Harrods kept a range of appliqué work on very fine linen. To promote sales in Britain, Beckett's had a subsidiary company, The Needlework Shop, with branches from Ipswich in the south to Scotland which stocked the full range of designs from the Fairistytch catalogue and a variety of other Art Needlework. (The Needlewoman Shop in Regent Street, London, was an outlet for Coats products, including Briggs.) Briggs and some other companies had similar part-colour catalogues from which customers could choose a design in a shop or purchase a copy, but not Deighton's. For many years they relied on a cheaply produced black and white booklet kept near a needlework counter and eventually added a coloured cover commissioned from a commercial artist. The names given to embroidery designs were extraordinary: some people had a talent for thinking up an infinite number at will — although few had any connection with the pattern Arenga, Pastolet, Verina, Geralda, ...!

Each piece of Fairistytch embroidery always included a comprehensive list of threads, stitches and a coloured photograph, 'No customer guessing involved', according to Mr E T Beckett who supplied much of the information about his company. Unconsciously, Mr Beckett had repeated the sentiments of Lady Alford, first Vice-Principle of the Royal School of Art Needlework, 'Nothing should be left to the imagination of the stitcher'! Deighton's rarely recommended a particular brand of thread; Briggs settled with Clark's because of their company's interest, but Fairistytch considered the French threads of Cartier Bresson to be of superior quality, although slightly more expensive. When supplies dried up in 1939 they were replaced by Peri Lusta of Leek, Staffordshire. Fairistytch embroideries often recommended the full six strands of thread. An idiosyncrasy of Fairistytch, rarely seen elsewhere, was a decorative hem traced with a pattern to compliment the main design. (*fig 22*)

During the 1930s many firms produced novelties — matinée coats, aprons, blotters, covers for *Radio Times*, curtains, bedspreads and much more. These Fairistytch designs were quite different from their floral patterns and were not successful, neither was a range of pictures (*fig 74*), although unusual and rather attractive.

Manufacturers of traced linens produced various designs to match patterns on 'best' china teasets, the willow pattern outselling all others. Another popular idea was taken from Mason's dark blue and orange Ironstone china.

The 1939-45 war was a difficult time for everyone but Mr Beckett managed to survive in spite of 50% of his factory space being requisitioned for essential war work. He had served in the army from 1914-18 and regarded another European conflagration as inevitable, so from 1930 onwards he had stockpiled raw materials.

Mr T F Beckett died in 1950 and his son took over the business. Times changed: the plethora of flowers, almost the trademark of Fairistytch, went out of fashion and Art Needlework lost its appeal. Radio had boosted sales but television accelerated the company's demise in 1960.

Although Briggs, Deighton's and Fairistytch have left a few clues which prove they carried out all the processes to make hot-iron transfers and traced needlework, it is difficult to be dogmatic about scores of other makers' names connected with the craft. From the large number of awful transfers and weak embroideries it is obvious that there were many small businesses who entered the market without any skills and their demise is no loss, but there were exceptions (*fig 24*).

To be fair to the companies who manufactured Art Needlework and claimed to have invented something new, it is impossible to know who originated an idea. Briggs came up with several 'new ideas' that had been popular before they were in business, and rumours were rife about employees sent from one factory to another to spy. The Deighton family have supplied some information about three names. Webber learnt his trade at Deighton's and around 1930 took all his knowledge with him and set up WEBCO. Turner was also with Deighton's and left about the same time to go into partnership with Boynton as Boynton & Turner Transfers (*fig 25*). In the 1950s they rejoined the old firm to become Deighton, Boynton & Turner (DBT) for a few years.

Barchester   Waltham

24 'Fleur-de-lis' designs published by Vicars & Pourson Ltd 1939

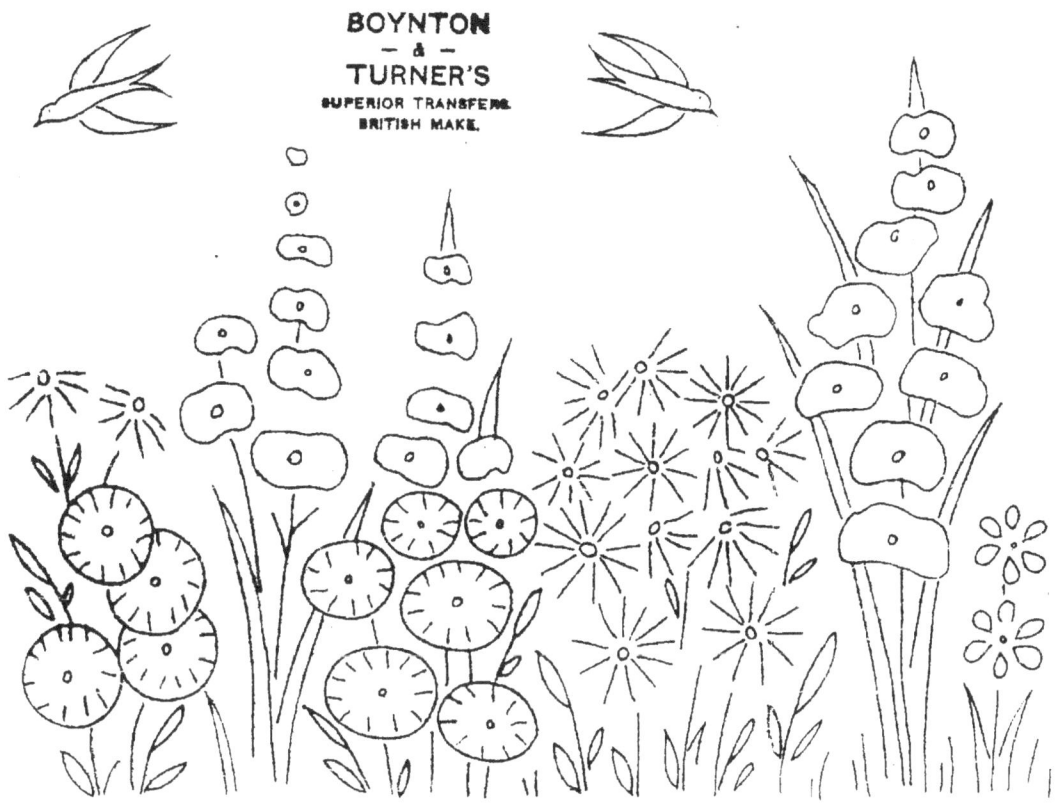

25: Transfer of part of a repeating border made by Boyton & Turner

Traced work and transfers sold by Old Bleach Linen Company, near Belfast, Northern Ireland were only partly made by them and it is not known if other companies used a similar method. The history of Old Bleach was published in a small promotional booklet and additional information has been provided by one of their employees.

In 1864 the company began to manufacture high quality linen cloth and became the largest of several mills which promoted embroidery. The name originated from their old fashioned method of bleaching linen by repeated exposure to the sun while laid out on grass. Their floral designs for household linens were drawn by ladies at the factory who understood how to obtain the correct effect on the various textures of linen. A perforation was then made and this was sent to Briggs for the transfers to be mass produced. Transfers and traced linens could be bought by mail order or at fancy work shops. Their annual catalogue had attractive Richelieu, broderie anglaise and crewel work patterns for white, écru and polychrome embroidery (*fig 26*). Embroideresses were employed at the factory to stitch by hand the bed and table linen for sale in high class shops. The standard of work was excellent and a close examination of the back is necessary to distinguish hand from machine-made embroidery (*fig 27*).

Although outside the subject of this book, during the 1930s Old Bleach produced

26: 4 Designs illustrated in *The Embroideress* 1933. Original drawing made at Old Bleach Linen Co. Randalstown, Northern Ireland; transfers mass-produced by Briggs

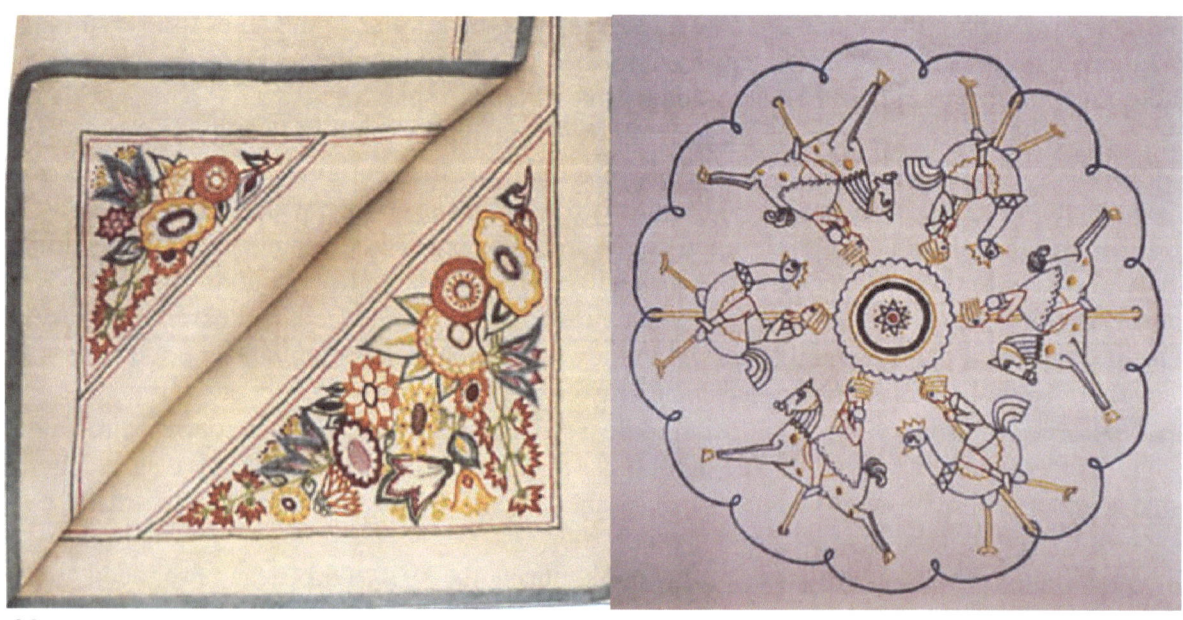

27. Pillowslip manufactured and hand-embroidered at Old Bleach Linen Co.
Design probably by Old Bleach Linen Co. Randalstown, N. Ireland.
For sale in high class shops. Transfers from Briggs.

exciting furnishing fabrics with very modern printed patterns for hotels, liners (including the *Queen Mary*), aircraft and the new and wonderful cinemas (especially *Odeons* with their Art Deco architecture).

Old Bleach linen was always of the best quality but the factory closed in 1970.

A glance through any lady's magazine from the turn of the century onwards will include numerous advertisements for traced linens, from small shops and large stores. There are vast quantities of old, embroidered linens — sheets, pillow slips, tablecloths, tray cloths, tea cosy covers, table runners, chair backs, duchesse sets — the list goes on and on. The quality varies, of course, but even the very best is still relatively inexpensive.

ART NOUVEAU, 1900-1920

The Arts and Crafts Society, founded in 1888, was devoted to decorative rather than fine art. The names of many of the artists are well known, for example William Morris, Edward Burne-Jones, Walter Crane and Lewis Day, but although some of their marked-out designs were available, for instance from Morris' workshop, and supplied to the Royal School of Art Needlework to be embroidered, nothing reached the popular market. Transfers with smocking dots were used by ladies who followed the Arts and Crafts rebellion against corsets and made loose-fitting, smocked garments.

    Liberty's department store in London opened in 1875 and sold new and imaginative transfers designed by leading artists who had to accept anonymity. An advertisement in 1883 offered, '100 original designs for transfers', and the following year a women's and children's department was opened with embroideresses in the workroom. The Deighton family believe that William Deighton sold his transfers to Liberty in the nineteenth century. Although there is no proof of this, they had introduced Celtic designs which complimented the *Cymric* and *Tudric* patterns on the metal ware and ceramics sold by Liberty, and Deighton's employed one or more artists who were very skilled at the Art Nouveau style so often linked with the store. By 1920 it is recorded that Deighton's made all the transfers sold by Liberty (stamped 'LIBERTY') (*fig 28*) and supplied smocking dots and other transfers for embroidering fashion garments in their workroom. A 1936 *Stitchcraft* magazine carried a Liberty advertisement for traced and commenced work but no transfers, which may have been discontinued.

    Although the names of artists who worked for Liberty were not acknowledged, one is known. Ann Macbeth, 1875-1948, trained at the Glasgow School of Art and sold her designs

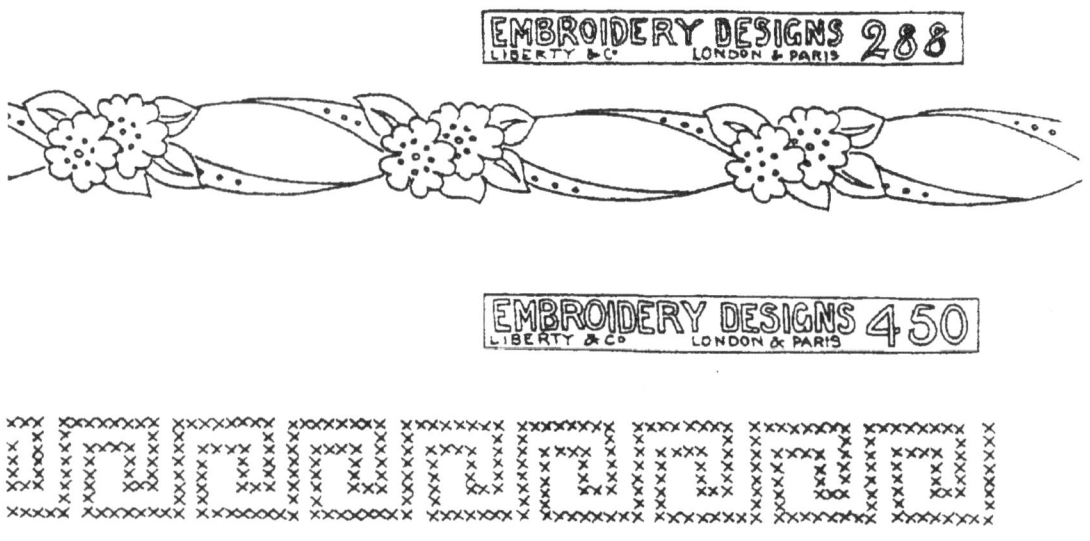

28. Liberty & Co transfers

Printed on paper size 20" x 20" (508mm x 508mm)
Celtic and Shamrock designs
When ordering please quote full reference

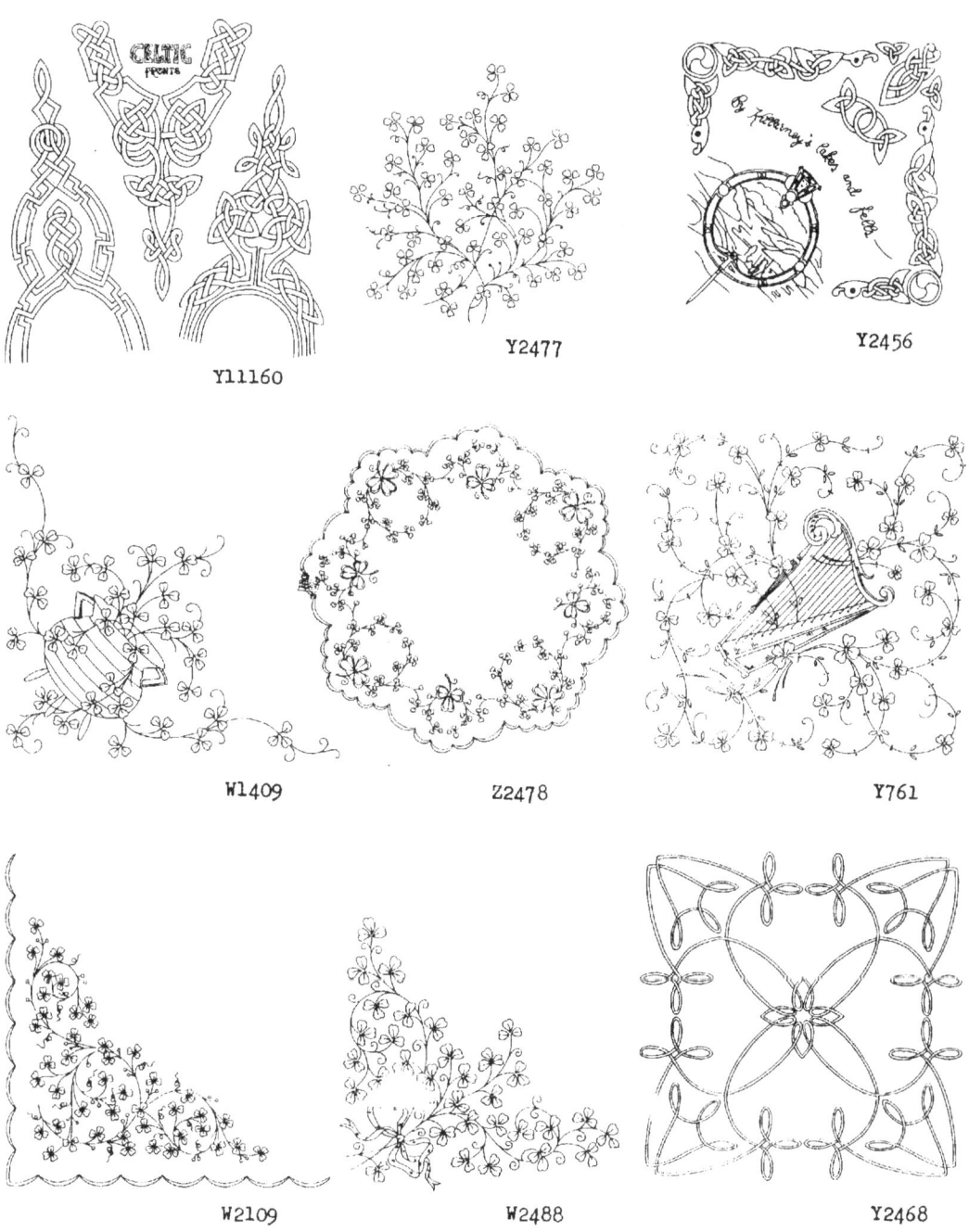

29: Copelands Linens Ltd. Belfast. Design still in production in 1990

to Knox Linen Thread Company and to Liberty. Ideas which originated at the Glasgow School of Art were to have a considerable influence on transfer designs from 1900-1920.

In 1885 Francis Newberry was appointed Principle of the Glasgow School of Art and under his guidance, together with his wife, Jessie, Charles René Mackintosh, Ann Macbeth and their associates, a new art form developed. Their ideas reached a large circle of interested people through a travelling exhibition and practical informative talks. It is very possible one or more of Deighton's artists saw or heard them. Briggs produced some designs in the new style, but they were not as prolific as Deighton's output.

The sinewy, twining plant form of Art

Cuckoo Pint.—CUSHION.

No. 4077.
Design 19¼ inches by 20 inches.

30: Briggs *Blanche Fitzmaurice Portfolio of Artistic Needlework* c1890
All Saints Library,
Manchester Metropolitan University

Columbine.—CUSHION.

Design 20¼ inches square.

31: Briggs *Blanche Fitzmaurice Portfolio of Artistic Needlework* c1890
All Saints Library,
Manchester Metropolitan University

Nouveau was at its height from 1890-1910. The *Briggs Blanche Fitzmaurice Portfolio of Artistic Needlework* published in the 1890s had a few patterns of plants in this style, e.g. cuckoo pint, columbine and chilli pepper with seed pods, but nothing else (*figs 30, 31, 32*). When, however, the extravagances of Art Nouveau began to wane with the arrival of Modern ideas, it eventually arrived at the commercial stage and many transfers were made between 1910 and 1920 — some much later. Without written evidence it is difficult to date them.

Deighton's produced the patterns and transfers for *Art Needlework Select and Original Designs*, published by the English Sewing Cotton Co Ltd during the reign of Edward VII, 1901-1910. The company manufactured Arderns,

Dewhurst (Sylko) and Bagley & Wrights 'new lustrous mercerised thread considerably cheaper than the silks used by The Royal School of Art Needlework'. Every design was beautifully embroidered and photographed in colour for the catalogue. Although one or two patterns were old-fashioned, typically Victorian, the majority were exciting Art Nouveau creations with exotic butterflies, peacocks and a variety of flowers including the pansy 'which suggests charming thoughts'. The designs were copyright and available from Art Needlework shops and drapers (*figs 33, 34, 35*).

Plant forms, based but not copied from natural flowers, leaves, stems and even roots, were very decorative when embroidered in soft yellows, pearly white, silver grey, pinks, powder blue, lavender and greens. There was a plethora of good reference books on plant studies, for example *Plant Form and Design*, A E V Lilley and W Midgley, was reprinted six times between 1896-1907.

32: *Briggs Blanche Fitzmaurice Portfolio of Artistic Needlework* c1890 All Saints Library, Manchester Metropolitan University

33 Table Centre. *Art Needlework Select and Original Designs*. Deighton's tracework. Published by English Sewing Cotton Co. Ltd. 1901-1910

34 Chairback - *Art Needlework Select and Original Designs*.
Deighton's tracework. Published by English Sewing Cotton Co. Ltd. 1901-1910

35 Sideboard Cloth - Traced work on coloured linen by Deighton's. Illustrated in
Art Needlework Select and Original Designs.
Published by English Sewing Cotton Co. Ltd. 1901-1910

36: *Glasgow Art School* style roses. Deighton's 1920s

The stylised rose, distorted and unnatural, is probably the most recognisable motif from the Glasgow School, especially when embroidered in Art Shades of greens, browns, pinks and white (*fig 36*). A 1911 edition of *The Lady's World Fancywork Book* featured designs of 'quaintly shaped roses worked on tan linen in shades of dull rose and greens with a pale blue ribbon' (*fig 37*), and a delightful coloured linen tablecloth embroidered in white with a border of flowers and butterflies. The magazine also had transfers for embroidered net and braid lace. The latter was a simple form of needle-made lace popular between 1875-1920, which used machine-made braid joined by bars and wheels, for table linen, bed covers, doilies and dress trimming. Large amounts of this lace are available and it is not advisable to buy any damaged pieces.

Deighton's Catalogue, 1910

Table covers	Mantle borders	Cushions
Sofa Cushions	Fire screens	Chair backs
Table centres	Piano cover	Work bag
Tray cloths	Sideboard cloths	Glove sachet
Tea cosies	Head rests	Towel ends
Blotter cover	Table cloths	Nightdress case

and designs suitable for blouses, dresses and collars.

Most of the floral patterns, little changed from Victorian times, were similar to a Briggs' catalogue, 1914.

A New Idea in "Salome" Work

THE conventional rose design always finds so much favour that we give an illustration of one of its latest developments as applied to an oblong cushion cover of fine tan linen. The three quaintly shaped roses are worked in four shades of Vicars' Brillianté, the dull rose range Nos. 40, 45, 46 and 47. The centre of the three large outer petals is in the lightest shade of all, those on either side of it in the next shade. Rose No. 40 is used for the pointed petal at the top, the three little solid dots below it and the curved petal to the right, while the rest of the petals are in the intermediate shades. Satin stitch is used throughout, the larger petals of the flowers and all the leaves being worked in two sections with stitches directed outwards from the centre. The greens employed are Nos. 49, 50 and 51, and the ribbon is treated with the pale soft blue No. 33. The small crescent shapes which form a kind of powdering are in the palest green, with a filling of French knots in rose No. 47. A black outline worked in filoselle gives character and finish to the design.

Salome Oblong Cushion.

37: Cushion *The Lady's World Fancywork Book* 1911

Fancy Needlework Illustrated, 1906-1955, was published by the Northern School of Art Needlework (*fig 38*). As with the Manchester School of Needlework it was not an educational establishment but an outlet for the English Sewing Cotton Co Ltd and promoted Deighton's transfers from an address in St Mary's Passage, Russell Street, Manchester, an alley near the prison, too small to be listed in a contemporary street directory. By 1912 the magazine could only be contacted through a Manchester box number, the same number given in Deighton's advertisement to obtain their catalogue or transfers by post. Deighton's never gave their London address. Each *Fancy Needlework Illustrated* included a photograph and instructions for

38: Cushion *Fancy Needlework Illustrated* 1912. Published by English Sewing Cotton Co. Ltd. As the Northern School of Art Needlework. Deighton's transfer.

six new embroideries for which a transfer with a certain identification number was available by post from the 'School', or an identical pattern with another number, attributed to Deighton's, could be obtained from fancywork shops.

Deighton's always advertised in *Fancy Needlework Illustrated*. In 1912 12,000 different designs were available, by 1920 25,000. Each advertisement showed a lady transferring a pattern with the back edge, not the sole, of a flat iron. The magazine had regular competitions for amateurs, including schools, for which the use of English Sewing Cotton threads was compulsory. The prizes were very small and actually decreased in value over the years, but a first prize of ten shillings (50p) was worth having.

Not all magazines were interested in Art Nouveau designs for embroidery, but some used them for other crafts. *Needle and Home — the Lady's Fancy Work Magazine*, c1912, a French publication translated into fair English (with six sheets of very dull transfers of no merit whatsoever), featured a blotter decorated with stylised roses and good lettering for painting *à la gouache*, and a splendid oak screen in the style of René Mackintosh, with a design of teasels for poker work. A 1914 *Weldon's Ladies' Journal* also had transfers suitable for embroidery or poker work on wood. Poker work was recommended as a suitable decoration on velvet and a description of the potentially very dangerous method appeared in *Everywoman's Encyclopaedia*, 1912. Deighton's produced many transfers between the wars for poker work, stencilling, wood carving and leather work.

The Women's Institute, founded in 1913, and the Townswomen's Guild, 1917, both encouraged original design but never objected to their members using transfers.

In 1907 or earlier *Weldon's Ladies' Journal* may have been the first publication to give away a free transfer. Pre-1910 free transfers fall into two groups: broderie anglaise and decorative scallops for under-linen or floral patterns and plants drawn from life which were suitable for coloured embroidery. The designs were very similar to those published by Briggs in the 1880s, which proves once again the difficulty of dating embroidery although, fortunately, many free transfers were dated (*figs 39, 40*).

In 1900, Briggs published the first of their successful series *Needlecraft Practical*

39: A very early free transfer made by Briggs

40. Free transfer. *Lady's World* 1914.

Journal from the Manchester School of Needlework (*fig 41*). Seven new subjects were added each year and kept in print indefinitely, the first free transfer with the name 'Briggs' was issued in 1911. These continued to 1922 when the journal evolved into the monthly *Needlecraft*, and in 1937 it merged with J&P Coats *Needlewoman* (started in 1922, and always with a free transfer). *Needlewoman and Needlecraft* ceased in 1965.

Regrettably, the artistic quality of the free transfer was frequently poor. The designs, not available elsewhere, were sometimes drawn by the transfer manufacturer but more frequently by anyone in the office of the promoter who thought they had a talent for art! The free transfer became a very popular marketing gimmick for countless magazines and a variety of unrelated products. (See Appendix for some of the publications and other products involved). The output was amazing. In the 1950s, when an alternative production method was used, *Women's Weekly* ordered one and a half million for insertion into four successive issues.

    The free transfer has contributed to much misunderstanding about the quality of all transfers. Most were not wanted, many were never liked but kept 'just in case'. Too many embroideries sewn from them are of poor workmanship and are unattractive; very few are representative of the best Art Needlework although among them are some that truly reflect the art of each period (*figs 40, 41, 42, 43, 44, 45*).

41: *Needlecraft Journal of Embroidery Shading,* 1907. Published by Briggs as the Manchester School of Needlework

42: Free Transfer *Weldon's Ladies' Journal* 1913.

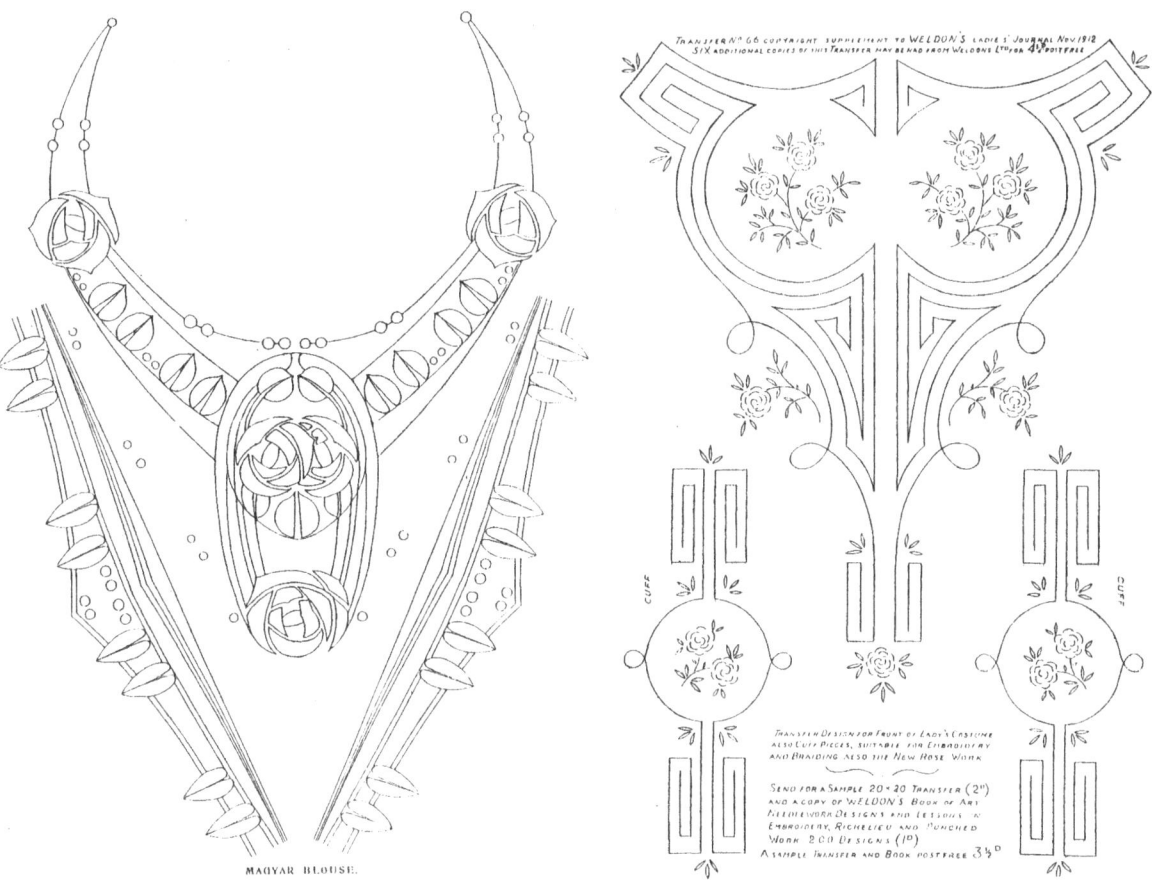

43: Blouse. *The Lady's World* supplement 1911. Gallery of English Costumes, Platt Hall, Manchester

44: Free transfer. *Weldon's Ladies' Journal* 1912. Gallery of English Costumes, Platt Hall, Manchester

45. Free Transfer *Weldon's Ladies' Journal* 1917.

ART DECO, 1920-1939

By 1914, Victorian taste was very old fashioned, although countless homes had sound furniture and furnishings that would last a lifetime and more. After the end of the war manufacturers of patterns for embroidery struggled to find something to attract customers and tried everything from medieval and Georgian to the olde-worlde cottage look, but little was new or exciting. Self-opinionated experts were scathing about the work of amateurs and some downright rude, 'Embroiderers without art school training find it hard to appreciate more advanced ideas, it is distressing to see people waste their time', *The Studio*; and 'Embroidery for most people means copying some past design or an even less intelligent method — that of transfer', the Embroiderers Guild. A few writers tried to encourage amateurs to design their own patterns, but did not condemn them if they did not. One was Mary Thomas, a popular writer on embroidery who thought transfers encouraged the art and made it accessible to all. The judges at an exhibition staged by the Women's Institute actually praised the high quality of embroideries based on transfers.

If an embroidery is worked by a skilled hand the result should be attractive, regardless of the origin of the pattern, one has only to look at the standard achieved in illustrated catalogues. However, the general public did not have access to expensive art books for inspiration and relied on their own taste for the choice of decorations in their homes. We must never forget, we choose what we like.

Before 1914, a few artists had experimented with Modern Art. Their ideas did not reach the home market, but soon after the war ended a geometric or abstract art form with vibrant colours of cerise, yellow, orange, violet, emerald and bright blues gradually found favour with some needlewomen. This was Jazz — a new style for a New Age. The name is sometimes used to describe the art of the 1920s and Modernism for the 1930s but today all vibrant art of the twenties and thirties is widely known as Art Deco.

The name is a contraction of the *Exposition des Arts Decoratifs et Industriels Modernes* held in Paris in 1925

46: Large design. Deighton's Transfer 1920s.

to show the work of the best designers from many countries. It was poorly supported by British industry who had promoted the *British Empire Exhibition* at Wembley the previous year. The comprehensive illustrated Paris catalogue confirmed that the few British exhibitors remained stoically traditional. In connection with the Exposition several volumes of Art Deco designs were available free of copyright to promote their use on wallpaper, ceramics, textiles, etc, and the manufacturers of transfers must have been aware of the new style, but, as usual they were reluctant to invest money in an unproven product. There were a few Art Deco embroidery transfers made pre-1920, slightly more in the twenties, but the majority were produced in the thirties. There was a real problem when designers produced eccentric ideas which would not fit easily into ordinary homes. The Royal Society of Arts tried to encourage students to keep in closer touch with manufacturers, '..... they are notoriously indifferent to the limitations imposed by the world of trade and the sooner they begin to face the facts underlying production, the better for all concerned.' The British Institute of Industrial Art criticised an exhibition at the Victoria and Albert Museum for 'the predominance of wall hangings and panels and the lack of useful tablecloths and bedspreads'. Many of these exhibitors had used transfers, mainly circular arrangements of brightly coloured flowers, although direct copies of old embroideries were prohibited (*figs 46, 47, 48*).

During the 1920s the Royal School of Art Needlework sold commenced needlework and transfers but no details have been discovered. It is possible the first transfers sold by the Embroiderers Guild were a collection bought in 1923 from A T Co and rubber-stamped 'Embroiderers' Guild AlphaBet (*sic*) Transfers', from 1926 they sold transfers manufactured by Deighton's but under their own name with designs taken from historical sources, the earliest 'modern' one was published in 1938.

47: Briggs Transfer 1930s

During the nineteenth century Berlin wool embroidery gave many women an opportunity to earn a meagre living and until 1914 Art Needlework, especially on bedspreads and portières, had offered similar work, but by the mid-1920s this trade had disappeared and skilled needlewomen joined the queues of the unemployed. This was partly due to the influence of fashionably bare rooms furnished in Art Deco style by the more affluent public.

The fashion for bare rooms, devoid of knickknacks was mentioned in *Good Housekeeping*, 1926, 'The dining table must be comely enough to endure the ordeal of bareness'. Old Bleach was less polite, 'The unfriendliness of the polished table with its forlorn little mats .....'. But there was a heavy price to pay for abandoning tablecloths and sideboard runners. Cheap furniture with shiny French-polished surfaces was sold on hire purchase at department stores and in smaller shops. It

48: Deighton's Transfer 1930s

49: Transfer of geometric designs. Deighton's 1931

appealed to customers with no experience of quality, but its pristine condition had a short life unless handled with great care. It was not long before cloths, runners and mats of shapes and sizes returned (*fig 49*).

Although Pearsall's had failed in 1907 with *Embroidery* and in 1914 with *Needle and Thread*, in 1925 they collaborated again with Old Bleach Linen Co Ltd to produce another high quality magazine which was successful: *The Embroideress*. Designs

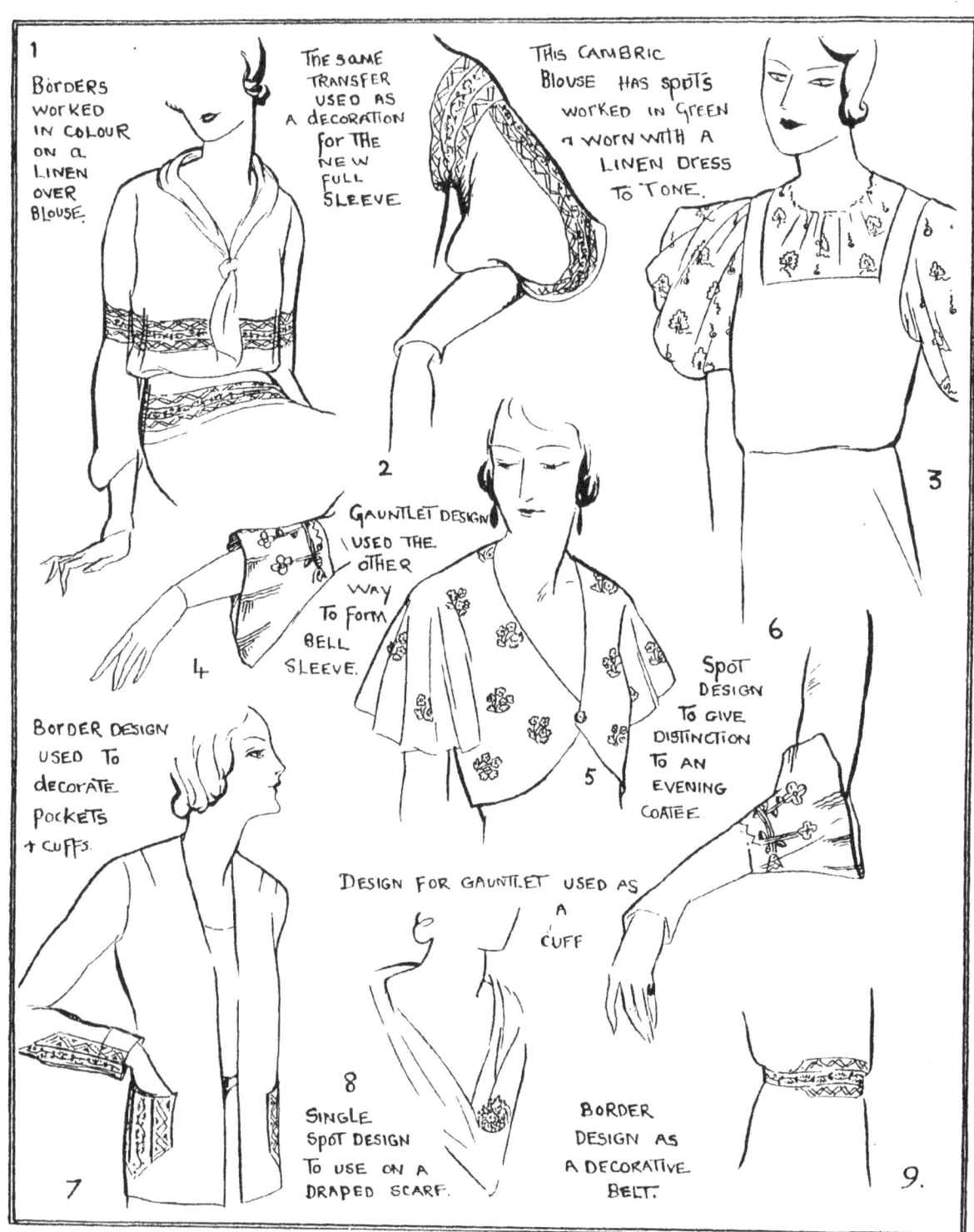

50: Ideas for Embroidery *The Embroideress* 1932

were modern but not abstract, the colours bright but not garish. The transfers were made by Briggs and were suitable for household linens and ladies' and children's wear — hat bands, glove gauntlets, sashes, etc (*figs 50, 51*). Pearsall's also published traditional designs under their own name and in 1926 probably held the first exhibition in London of 'Modern' needlework. The majority of the exhibitors were amateurs as professional embroideresses considered themselves artists and scorned such events!

By 1913 Briggs owned several adjoining properties in Cannon Street and a decision was taken to demolish and rebuild. Everything went according to plan, but the removal to an impressive modern building had been arranged for 3rd August 1914, the day before war was declared. All horses were requisitioned for war purposes and most of the moving had to be done by hand by Briggs' employees. *(The House of Briggs, F Briggs, 1951)*

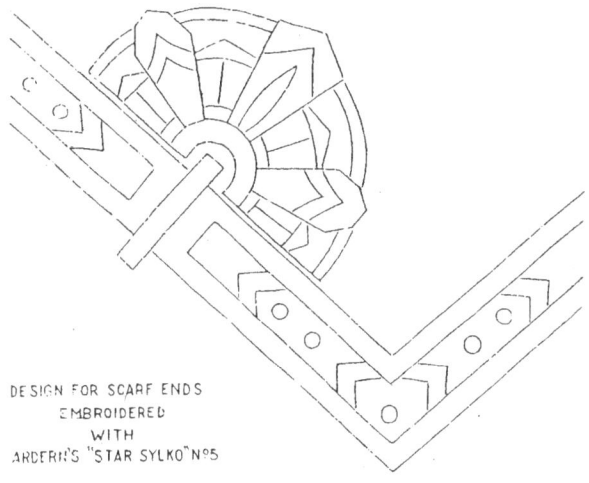

51: Typical Art Deco design Deighton's transfer 1930s

52: Free Transfer. *Stitchcraft* 1939

An employee of Briggs recalled their workroom in 1927:

"Six women and a senior produced the perforated designs which were despatched to a factory in Cheetham Hill to be mass produced. Small quantities of transfers were made from these by hand, with repeat orders if there was a demand. If any design did not sell well very few copies were ever made." [A fact to consider if attempting to find a particular subject of a needle etching, for example.]

A specimen of every design was stitched and sent to the Palantine Press to be photographed. This firm had printed Briggs' catalogues, leaflets and other publications from 1900. Briggs later became part-owners and bought the company in 1948.

The question of what type of embroideries to collect from the 1920s and 1930s is difficult to answer but, as always, collect what appeals to you — never for investment. *Figs 52, 53, 54, 55, 56, 57* are good examples of Art Deco transfers given away in magazines.

The imaginative, though not always popular, contemporary work from art schools is rarely seen, often expensive and outside the scope of this book.

Many middle class families were drawn to 'Tudor' ideas and there is an over-abundance of 'Jacobean' embroidery which is still popular today, although an acquired taste.

53: Art Deco motifs for costume. Various early 1930 magazines

54: Free transfer. *Needlework Illustrated* Briggs Transfer 1930s

STITCHCRAFT FEBRUARY 1935.

55: Free transfer. *Stitchcraft* 1935

Surprisingly, the 'blue collar' artisans more readily accepted Art Deco into their homes than the middle classes. This was probably due to the influence of the cinema. Going to the pictures was a frequent and cheap pastime where the glamorous and modern life-style was far removed from their own. Eventually inexpensive linoleum, rugs, wallpaper, china and textiles with modern designs appeared in the High Street.

Regrettably, much of the embroidery sewn at this time was poor quality, linked to the general economic situation and in particular to the changes in life-style. Before 1914 splendid work was accomplished by skilled amateur embroideresses, who were paid for their efforts, or stitched by the wives and daughters of businessmen who had an abundance of leisure time. After the war everything changed. More women went out to work and those at home without servants were busy with cooking, cleaning, shopping and looking after the children. There was less time for intricate needlework and embroidery had to be 'effective but quick, not put a strain on the worker'.

56: Free transfer. *The Needlewoman* mid-1930s. Briggs

STITCHCRAFT SEPTEMBER 1939

57: Free transfer. *Stitchcraft* 1939.

By 1930, all crafts were at a low ebb but attitudes changed with the introduction of the wireless. Men and women could sit down after tea and listen while they used their hands for modelling, rug making, knitting, crochet, embroidery and much more — but rarely was it fine stitchery and most ladies still preferred something pretty which Art Deco certainly was not. Constance Howard, an authority on needlework as art, had little to say in favour of transfers but she wrote, 'For my birthday in 1923 my mother made me a dress the bodice of which was completely covered with a large basket of flowers — a transfer for a square cushion — I thought it was elegant' (*fig 58*).

Between the wars certain subjects on transfers were typical of the period, great fun, and complimentary to the styles of the furniture, ceramics, glass, etc which have become so collectable today. There were many aspects of speed, for example leaping deer, electric flashes, sunbursts, men and women with straight or zigzag hair flying the wind, express trains, racing cars, boats and

58: Bodice for wedding dress made in 1990 using earlier transfers

even aircraft. It was a time for fresh air and exercise away from the towns with family beach holidays, skiing in the mountains, playing tennis or hiking (*figs 59, 60, 61, 62, 63*).

59: Free transfer *Stitchcraft*

60: Free transfer. *Weldon's Ladies' Journal* 1931

Many pictorial subjects were embroidered in outline only but they usually have a feeling of the period. However, one must be careful in dating Art Deco designs as they may be much later than they appear, for example, in 1945 *Needlewoman and Needlecraft* used a leaping deer attributed to Lady Smith-Dorrien, Principle of the Royal School of Needlework. The joy of much Art Deco embroidery is the wonderful colour.

61: Free transfer. *Needlewoman* 1937 (the definite article has been dropped). Briggs

62: The Emroideress 1931
Briggs transfer,
Old Bleach,
Ireland design

FIGURE 1517.—FULL SET OF DESIGNS FOR A BOY'S ROOM OF WHICH TRANSFERS ARE AVAILABLE.

63: Typical sunburst Art Deco design from the 1930s

NEEDLE ETCHINGS and other PICTURES

Between 1780 and 1830 there was a fashion among ladies with plenty of time and patience to embellish small etchings printed on silk by embroidering every line with a straight stitch in fine black, brown or grey silk thread, very occasionally a little human hair was introduced which has given them the misleading name of 'hair pictures'. Sometimes water colour paint was added to enhance the sky or other features but due to ageing the pigment has usually degraded to shades of brown. The idea was revived for a short time around 1860 on slightly larger pictures with the use of additional French knots or seeding. Only a relatively small number of print-work pictures (the correct name) were embroidered and they have become expensive collectors' items.

During the early 1930s William Briggs began to manufacture needle etchings, which had the appearance of steel engravings, stamped on to ecru linen or cotton. Every line was embroidered with one strand of sepia stranded cotton. Briggs claimed to be the originator of this type of needlework but it had many similarities to the earlier print work and some were even tinted. In the 1930s Briggs never sold transfers of these designs although Deighton's did. It has not been possible to find the exact date when either company commenced production.

64: Needle etching manufactured by Briggs 1930s—1960s.

Pre-1939 most of Briggs' etchings were sold on a light plywood mount which facilitated ease of working and simplified framing. The finished picture either had the glass taped cheaply in place with passe-partout or else the glass was held in place by a narrow brown or black wooden frame. A mount was never supplied during or after the war.

65 and **66**: Needle etchings manufactured by Briggs 1930s—1960s.

Briggs' lady artists worked from photographs to produce enlarged, accurate drawings. During the 1930s these were all topographical views of well-known landmarks throughout the British Isles. They were probably taken from picture postcards which were readily available for every location. The size of the embroidery, not the mount, was usually 7½ x 10 inches (19 x 25 cm). New titles were added continuously (*figs 64, 65, 66, 67*).

During the war a limited range was available for occupational therapy, but when rationing ended about five hundred titles were put on the market and became best sellers. A few new subjects appeared including breeds of dog and tall-masted ships.

67: Needle etching manufactured by Briggs 1930s—1960s.

Because of the obvious attraction of needle etchings, a list of Briggs' titles is given in the Appendix but it may not be complete.

As usual the artists were never identified but it is possible to distinguish the work of one lady from another using certain clues. For example, her way of drawing clouds or choice of lettering for the subject's title under the lower edge of the embroidered rectangular frame.

As already mentioned, Briggs copied another idea from print work and produced a few subjects tinted by the artist in sepia ink. The earliest date from about 1935 but they were not very popular and were discontinued in 1939 which was a pity (*fig 70*), as Briggs' *Old English Inns* were attractive. Most, if not all, of the hostelries are still open

68: Needle etching 'Pekinese' 1950s Briggs

69 Needle etching dated 1951, Briggs.

One of a pair worked by a man in Chatham, Kent, using an unusual technique.

70 Needle etching hand-tinted by a Briggs' artist but not worked. 1930s.

but many will have been extended or altered. The delightful pictures are difficult to find, the complete list is in the Appendix.

At a similar period, following a popular Chinese art exhibition in London, there was a small issue of tinted Chinese scenes.

Also during the 1930s Briggs produced maps for every county in the British Isles, with the coastline and county border tinted and the Coat of Arms, principle towns and rivers to be embroidered. There are a variety of embroidered maps about, but because of the tinting it is possible to identify and date those made by Briggs — if you are lucky enough to find one! A written account about maps embroidered by the long-term disabled servicemen during the Depression of the 1920s cannot be verified or the place of origin confirmed, but it is said they were the fifty-four *Maps of England* drawn by John Speed (1542-1629) which are full of intricate details; unless they had been simplified they would have been extremely difficult, even for an experienced hand. *The Embroideress*, 1933, emphasised the educational value of an embroidered map and Deighton's produced some transfers, but they were more decorative than geographically accurate.

The transfers Deighton's made for 'needle etchings' date from 1935 or earlier and were called simply 'embroidered pictures'. A Deighton's transfer of Windsor Castle, a free gift with *Women's Friend*, October 1935, and another of Stirling Castle, were almost identical views to those made by Briggs, which supports the theory that they were copied from picture postcards. Every subject used by Deighton's was also in the Briggs' range, but because of the scarcity of Deighton's catalogues it is not possible to know which were produced first. Deighton's never had such a comprehensive range as Briggs, and although most were sold as transfers, there were probably some ready-traced. A general catalogue, which the Deighton's family date from the early 1930s, offered five pictures; Durham Cathedral, Glamis Castle, Windsor Castle, St Paul's Cathedral and Tower Bridge. By 1950 others had been added, including Westminster Abbey, London Bridge, Balmoral, Canterbury Cathedral and The Old Curiosity Shop, London. A special etching of the Houses of Parliament, with a border of the national flowers of Great Britain and the Commonwealth, commemorated the Coronation of Queen Elizabeth II in 1952.

After the war Briggs made a few transfers for etchings but they were less attractive than their range of ready-traced, for example, two narrow rustic scenes to decorate a calendar, a cover for *Radio Times* given away with *Needlewoman and Needlecraft*, October 1945, and six heads of dogs in another edition.

In 1996 a few transfers were still for sale, including Windsor Castle, Tower Bridge and The Old Curiosity Shop. Unfortunately, they are badly drawn and printed in silver ink by Briggs, although labelled 'Deighton's'.

During the 1920s Briggs produced a new kind of picture with the design fully painted for customers to add embroidered details, usually foreground flowers. Each picture measured 9½ x 7 inches (24 x 18 cm) on fine natural-coloured cambric. They were either romantic views of the countryside with cottage gardens brimming with roses, hollyhocks and lupins or the grounds of a grand estate with lawns sweeping down to a river. In Briggs' workroom the original drawing was made into a transfer and stamped on to fabric and then taken to a nearby studio in Market Street where artists painted the whole picture.

Promotional examples were worked by the 'girls' at Briggs. The few pictures from the 1920s that can be positively dated are not of great artistic merit, the drawings are poor and the painting (probably water colour with Chinese white) crude and careless. Only the embroidery was well done (*figs 71, 72*). They must have sold, however, in sufficient numbers for in the 1930s Briggs increased the range and improved the quality.

71 and **72**: Two views hand-painted in watercolours with embroidered details. Briggs 1920s

73: Painted in poster paints with embroidered details Briggs 1930s

Artists, trained at the Manchester College of Art, were employed in the workroom and each painted her own work with bright poster paints (*fig 73*). Although some people prefer more muted shades, vibrant colours have always been popular with other families. The new range was made in three sizes, one suitable for a firescreen, stamped on to fine cotton and mounted on a wooden frame. Eight pictures were illustrated in Briggs' *Art Needlework Catalogue,* 1935:

Embroidery Size		Frame Size		Subjects
Imperial (ins)	Metric (cm)	Imperial (ins)	Metric (cm)	
7¼ x 4½	18 x 11.5	10 x 7½	25 x 19	Thatched cottage in rural landscape Timber framed cottage in garden
4 x 5	10 x 13	10 x 7½	25 x 19	Interior with open window Interior with open door
3¾ x 5¼	9.5 x 14	10 x 7½	25 x 19	Thatched Cottage in garden Crinoline lady in garden
5¾ x 8¾	15 x 22	10 x 12½	25 x 32	Thatched cottage by lake Thatched cottage in garden

A few superior oval pictures on silk were mounted on card, 5½ x 3¾ inches (14 x 9.5 cm).

No hand-painted pictures were manufactured after 1939 but recently some gifted needlewomen have re-introduced the craft with original designs.

Fairistytch produced a few pictures during the 1930s. Most can be identified by an original use of darning stitches over large areas of the embroidery such as the sky, fields or a lake; the designs were occasionally stamped on cushions. They have a certain charm. Samples were framed and sent to retail outlets to tempt customers, a shop in Keswick had several on display which were eventually given to the owner who commented that her customers were not very interested in working pictures and preferred something more useful.

Briggs and Deighton's made over a hundred designs for miniature embroideries which make an ideal collection for someone with insufficient room to display anything larger. They vary from minute flowers, ½ inch (12 mm) across, intended for earrings, to various patterns for brooches (*fig 75*), and little pictures no more than 6-7 inches (15-18 cm) across. Many other designs were tiny but intended for lingerie, etc.

74: 'Sunset' Fairistytch 1930s Embroidered in Madeira to use for a display in an Art Needlework shop in Keswick Lake District

Some miniature brooches were displayed at an exhibition of the British Institute of Industrial Art at the Victoria and Albert Museum in 1922. The embroideries were mounted in silver frames, one inch in diameter and obviously unusual. A copy of *The Needlewoman*, 1932, illustrated a crude idea using a curtain ring as a base, and at a similar date Liberty were embroidering buttons. During the 1939-45 war a shortage of all materials caused costume jewellery to be made from practically anything — embroidery, seeds and even sealing wax.

75: Miniature embroidered brooches Briggs 1950s

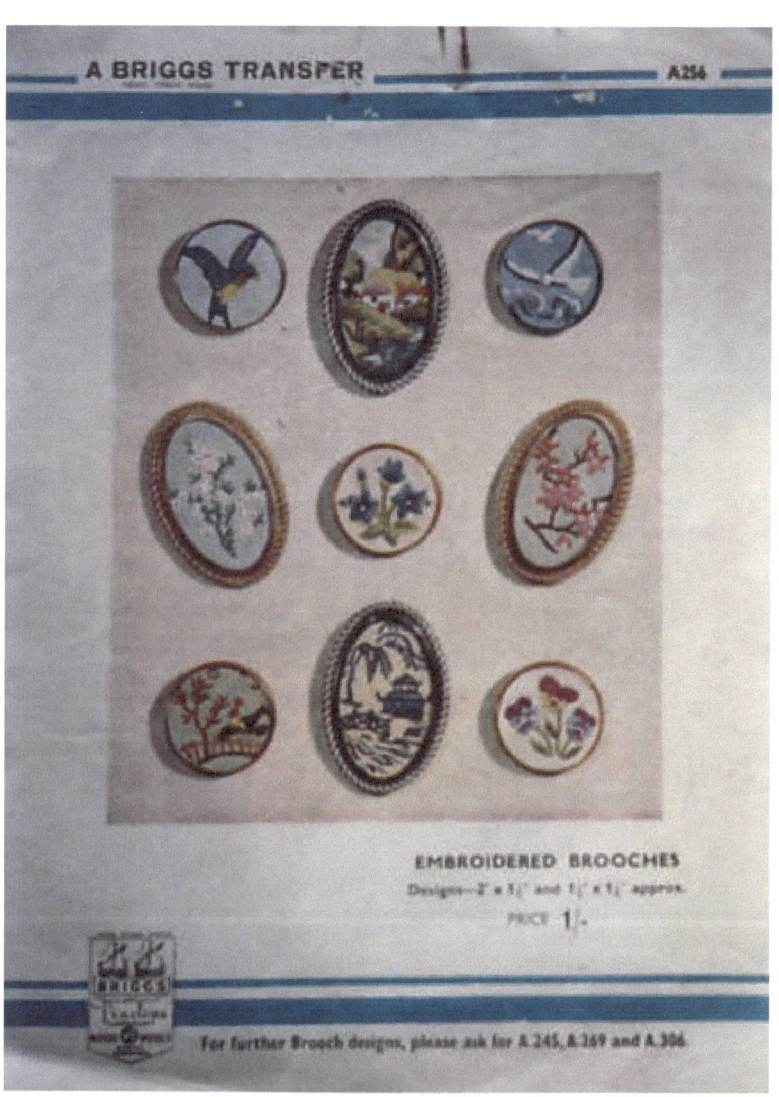

76: Leaflet with transfers for embroidered brooches Briggs 1950s– 1960s

Transfers for miniature work were available in the 1940s, throughout the 50s and maybe later.

Briggs' and Deighton's miniature designs on embroidered brooches are not uncommon (*fig 76*). They can be found among small, inexpensive antiques in their original metal frames of silver or gold coloured metal with a rope or plain edge. Most designs were floral with an occasional butterfly, bird, animal, cottage, one jolly golliwog and the inevitable crinoline ladies. For collectors of royal souvenirs both firms issued designs, no larger than 2 x 1¼ inches (5 x 3 cm), for the coronation in 1953 with portraits of the Queen, national emblems, well known royal castles and other landmarks. One designer is known, Wilfred Grove, a commercial artist living in Bristol who worked on commission for Deighton's which had premises located in the city at that time. Grove also produced three ideas for a Deighton's Art Needlework catalogue with a coloured cover, but his main income came from designing Christmas cards.

77, 78, 79, 80 : Miniature pictures in original frames 1950s Briggs

81, 82: Miniature pictures in original frames 1950s Briggs

Miniature pictures are more elusive. The following were available from Briggs during the 1950s:

Embroidery Size		Subjects	
Imperial (ins)	Metric (cm)		
4¾ x 3¾	12 x 9.5	In felt appliqué Spring (*fig 83A*) Summer (*fig 83B*)	Autumn (*fig 83C*) Winter (*fig 83D*)
3¼ x 2¼	8 x 6	Spring Summer Autumn Winter Lakeside Seascape (2)	Cottage and garden Village Church Hamlet Poppies Nasturtiums Bowl of Flowers (2)
6 x 6 circular	15 x 15 circular	Dovecote (*fig 81*) Water pump (*fig 82*)	Watermill Windmill Caravan

After 1960 the sizes varied slightly but remained small with additional designs, including a garden vista, wild duck, stage coach, the Waits, Homestead, Dutch interior, Holy Night and the Three Wise Men.

83 A to D (above) Miniature felt pictures Spring, Summer, Autumn and Winter 1956 Briggs

Appliqué felt pictures were offered as transfer designs in some catalogues and magazines (*fig 84*), but completed pictures are rare.

84: Felt picture 1960. Briggs

69

85, 86: Two pictures (16x 20cm) in
The Embroideress 1932,
the first suitable for a telephone book cover.
Briggs transfer on Old Bleach Linen

87: 'Country Scene'
Needlewoman & Needlecraft 1953 Briggs

OCCUPATIONAL THERAPY

During the 1914-18 war there was an active plan to provide various manual occupations to hasten the recovery of wounded and shell-shocked men in military hospitals (*fig 88*).

88: Wounded soldiers at Brookdale Military Auxiliary Hospital
V.A.D. Alderley Edge. *Fancy Needlework Illustrated* (Deightons) circa 1916

      It is not known who instigated the idea of offering needlework for its therapeutic value, but Constance Howard's *Twentieth Century Embroidery* suggested a few names. Ernest Thesiger, CBE, 1879-1961, an artist, embroiderer and successful actor, found solace in canvas work while recovering from war wounds and later started a scheme for which he designed canvases for soldiers in hospital. Ann Macbeth, a teacher at Glasgow School of Art, sent one of her students to a Reading hospital to introduce needlework and painting of pottery, and may have arranged similar activities elsewhere. Louisa Pesel, 1870-1947, an Inspector of Art Needlework and designer of canvas embroideries for Winchester Cathedral, helped to start a handicraft section in the Khaki Club, Bradford. Other organisers of occupational therapy were members of various handicraft guilds which had sprung up after 1900 to promote Art Needlework as a hobby.
      It is difficult to identify work made as occupational therapy. Owners of family pieces should endeavour to attach to the textile (without pins, please) as much information as possible, but there are some clues for collectors from the relatively small number of embroideries that can be dated accurately.
      Examples in the Imperial War Museum made during the 1914-18 war were all stitched with twisted embroidery silks. Those made from 1930 onwards, including the 1939-45 war,

all used stranded embroidery cotton. In spite of some horrendous injuries all the needlework was worked to a high standard showing the determination of the men and the skill of their teachers.

The Imperial War Museum has two large embroideries, from the First World War, suitable for a cushion or screen but not made up. One depicts a lion standing on white cliffs with allied flags, stitched on cheap natural-coloured cotton by Cpl Munday while recovering from wounds at Fort William Hospital, Scotland. The origin of this design is unknown but the other piece came from Deighton's with a design of roses and the words *Roses of Picardy* worked on black sateen by a soldier in the Royal Victoria Hospital, Netley, Hampshire (*fig 89*). It is possible that both these designs were available to the general public and not produced especially for servicemen as patriotic transfers were made at various times. *Weldon's Ladies' Journal*, December 1914, included a free transfer of British, French, Belgian and Russian flags and later gave away one to commemorate Alexandra Rose Day. Queen Alexandra, widow of Edward VII, had initiated a flag day to benefit nurses who tended the wounded. In 1940 the same magazine had a design with the popular wartime song 'Run! Rabbit, Run!'.

During the 1914-18 war, regimental badges were available for servicemen to embroider. The designs were very accurate and probably drawn and a sample stitched at the Royal School of Art Needlework who were experienced at similar work. So far, no record of the manufacturer has been found but it was probably Briggs. The range of badges available included most of the United Kingdom regiments and some from Canada, Australia and Transvaal, each design approximately 5 cm square. The Imperial War Museum has a collection of badges (*fig 90*), worked on scraps of cloth in a great variety of colour, size and texture, which probably came from the Royal School of Art Needlework. They have no provenance but the museum believe they were donated in 1917 when the government

89: Cushion cover worked as occupational therapy 1916 at Netley Royal Hospital, Hampshire.
Deighton's Transfer - Imperial War Museum

90 Regimental badges 1914-1918. Possibly samples worked at Royal School of Art Needlework and given to the Imperial War Museum in 1917 in response to the government's request to collect war-time memorabilia

(Top)
Royal Navy

Durham Light Infantry

Durham Light Infantry

Gloucestershire Regiment

Seaforth Highlanders

Canada

20th Hussars

The Monmouth Regiment

decided to collect and display material relating to the war. The regiments in the Imperial War Museum are:

Royal Warwickshire Regiment	Prince of Wales Regiment	Royal Engineers
Gloucestershire Regiment	Royal Army Medical Corps	Seaforth Highlanders
Monmouthshire Regiment	Royal Dublin Fusiliers	Royal Irish Rifles
Northamptonshire Regiment	Somerset Light Infantry	17th Lancers
North Staffordshire Regiment	Durham Light Infantry	20th Hussars

Oxford and Buckinghamshire Light Infantry

The Royal Flying Corps (made between 1912 and 1918, as after this date it became the Royal Air Force) has been added from another source. There were almost certainly more regimental badges available, but no record has been found of them.

Various badges made into pictures or firescreens can be found in antique shops but unless they are dated it is difficult to know when they were made. Regimental histories are a helpful source of information.

Unhappily, the plight of many ex-servicemen did not end with the Armistice and it was not uncommon to see severely disabled men busking or begging in the streets. This prompted Weldon's to publish an unusual transfer with a political message: the six 'Louis Wain' type cats (sold in a green envelope printed with instructions, as was usual at the time) had one holding a placard, 'Blind — kind friends, I am an English cat.'..... his staring eyes are sightless (*Fig 91*). Some disabled ex-servicemen relied on charities to provide remunerative employment, including needlework. It was offered for sale at bazaars and other venues patronised by a sympathetic and wealthy public. Each year, for example, a stall at the Chelsea Flower Show sold garden cushions and aprons embroidered with brightly coloured wools, and periodic sales at the Imperial Institute included various household linens, numerous bags and pincushions.

Between the wars a few badges designed by the Royal School of Needlework were marketed by Briggs for the home market. Each was sold in a folder, in a cellophane wrapper, with a coloured picture and two transfers, small, 3½ inches (9 cm) square, and large, 7 or 9 inches (18 or 23 cm) square (*figs 92, 93, 94*). On the reverse of the folder was a brief history of the regiment by Lieut Cdr E C Talbot-Booth RNR and a list of the badges available. The earliest list had eighty names but they were not numbered or in any

91: Weldon's Transfer Patterns
An unusual transfer publicising the plight of disabled servicemen

particular order, beginning: Royal Dragoons, Scots Greys, Grenadier Guards, etc.

From about 1940 the list was numbered but the regiments were in the same order starting No 1 Royal Dragoons. A few badges, together with a history of the regiment, were featured in *The Needlewoman* during the 1930s. Transfers that could be bought from shops, included: The Black Watch, Royal Artillery, Royal Navy, Coldstream Guards, Royal Air Force, Royal Northumberland Fusiliers, Seaforth Highlanders and the Royal Engineers.

Soon after the declaration of war in 1939 the number of regimental and other badges began to increase and by 1942 there were one hundred and thirty, including the Land Army, and Canadian and American insignia. A complete list is given in the Appendix.

Materials for the home market became extremely scarce and all textiles were rationed, but a small quantity of

92, 93, 94 (next page): Briggs probably between the wars and possibly later. Each packet contains two transfers. Note: varying size of packets, probably due to paper shortages.

transfers for badges were manufactured for the home market to keep up morale. Neither Briggs nor Deighton's could have survived the war years, albeit with a reduced staff, without supplementary products. Briggs embroidered naval officers' cap badges and Deighton's insignia for the army, and both benefited from the official Occupational Therapy Embroidery Scheme. They acquired a licence from the Board of Trade to obtain fabric without coupons and used it to purchase cloth and prepare traced linens for hospital patients and HM Forces at sea or in isolated stations. Items made included both crests, and designs from Deighton's and Briggs' regular catalogues.

94 (above)

The embroideries were distributed exclusively by British, Canadian and American Red Cross Society hospitals, Army Educational Units, Welfare Units of the Royal Navy, Royal Air Force, Women's Royal Naval Service, Auxiliary Territorial Service and the Women's Auxiliary Air Force. Unfortunately no records were kept, but in All Saint's Library, Manchester Metropolitan University there is a Briggs' catalogue, *Needlecraft for the Forces*, from which much of this information has been taken (*fig 96*) The badges

95: Worked on very poor quality cotton as occupational therapy 1941-43 by a man recovering from an injury received while serving with the invasion deception plan.
Briggs. Imperial War Museum

96: c1939-40. All Saints Library, Manchester Metropolitan University

(called 'crests' on the transfers) were all approved by the War Office and stamped (ready traced) on to beige crash for fire screens, cushion covers and table runners, or cream cotton for pictures.

From 1939-42, Joyce Grenfell, broadcaster and actress and related to Viscount Astor of Clivedon on whose estate she lived, was a regular helper at a local military hospital that cared for Canadian and British casualties. Among her duties she taught needlework to the patients. She referred to this as 'handicrafts' until 1942 when she was informed that henceforth it was to be known as 'occupational therapy'.

> "I've taught more new patients than ever before. They are so touching, stitching away. I've managed to get some lovely, plain coloured tray cloths and on these I put their crests and set them off to work in coloured threads. Some of them do really wonderful work ..... finer than any woman ..... it's quite extraordinary to see the good effects sewing has on them. They get an interest and forget their ailments. The docs encourage it, particularly in the cases where the men have to be in bed for long times. August 2nd 1942". *Darling Ma, Hodder & Stoughton, 1988.*

Although embroidery was enjoyed by many service personnel, there was a problem, particularly with the regimental badges and a set of six pictures. The close stitching needed to be worked in a frame to obtain a satisfactory result (several of the embroideries from 1914-18 at the Imperial War Museum were worked this way and the marks of the frame can be seen). Briggs optimistically suggested a frame could be made from odd pieces of wood which was not practical in the circumstances, but someone came to the rescue. An appeal for frames was launched in the *Daily Telegraph*, November 1942 with a tremendous response from the public.

For anyone interested in embroidered badges of the 1939-45 war, Briggs published in 1940 *Badges of HM Services - a History of Badges, Regimental Standards, Guidons and Colours*, by Major T J Edwards, MBE, FRHisS. It was reprinted several times. The Imperial War Museum has a leather-bound presentation copy with a typewritten letter from 34 Cannon Street, Manchester (Mr Briggs?) attached: 'Briggs & Co Ltd dedicate this book to every family with a representative in HM Forces and offer it as a record of history for centuries to come.' The writer went on to thank Lady Smith-Dorrien, Principle of the Royal School of Needlework, for the great help given by her and her staff, the author and his assistant, F C Bowen Esq. In the foreword Major Edwards explained why the special features in the life of the regiments were important. The book was well-written and worth reading, if a copy can be found. To give just one example:

'Somerset Light Infantry

This was raised in 1682. The original purpose of Light Infantry was to act quickly in advance of the main army during active operations. In order to do this they had to march quicker and lighter than ordinary infantry and a drum was too cumbersome so Light Infantry worked to a bugle in the field. Light Infantry regiments always March Past at quick pace and wear a bugle as part of their badge. The mural Crown superscribed 'Jellalabad' epitomises the regiment's distinguished conduct during the First Afghan War, 1839-42. It held Jellalabad against fifty times their number ..... Queen Victoria approved 'Prince Albert's' to be added to the title, the 'PA' on the strings of the bugle ..... the Queen also granted the badge of a Mural Crown as a memorial to their fortitude, perseverance and enterprise. HM the King is Colonel-in-Chief of the Regiment.'

For more experienced hands a set of six? embroidered pictures was available, similar to designs occasionally offered in *The Needlewoman* during the 1930s. Not all have been identified but J2 is Anne Hathaway's Cottage, J5 a Rose Garden and J6 a Manor House. Each embroidery measured 10 x 7½ inches (25 x 19 cm) and various stitches completely covered the background material. Although each piece of work came with several pages of instructions, the method, as used in *The Needlewoman,* of linking a code on a black/white drawing with particular colours and stitches, is difficult to follow in spite of a very small coloured photograph of the finished work and a full size black/white one of a detail.

The illustrations on the next three pages are the instruction leaflet for Anne Hathaway's Cottage. (All Saints Library, Manchester Metropolitan University)

Although very difficult to identify, the most popular embroideries with service personnel were Deighton's and Briggs' Art Needlework designs for table runners, chair backs and cushion covers in crash, and table cloths in various sizes, tray cloths and tea napkins on cream cotton, all with traditional floral designs - something useful to send back home (and a way of getting table linen without coupons) (*fig 100*). Briggs' illustrated catalogue of their full range of occupational therapy embroideries had eight pages of stencilled canvases, two each of traced pictures and needle etchings and five for regimental badges, but there were so many Art Needlework designs for household furnishings that there was only one page of general information without any details of patterns.

Most of Briggs' kits for servicemen during World War 2 was supplied in a brown paper folder to use as a container while the work was in progress. It held the material with neatened edges and was stamped with a design, a small coloured picture and contained an instruction chart, only 10 cm square because of the shortage of paper but, 'explicit enough to allow anyone not skilled in embroidery to achieve a pleasing result'. In the folder there were also two needles and sufficient skeins of Anchor stranded cotton to finish the work. Although the Deighton family know something similar was produced by them, no records

NEEDLECRAFT for H.M. FORCES

Produced by

UNDER BOARD OF TRADE LICENCE Nos. 1151/1/M5/305. 1103/M5/4096. 1151/1/M5/2711.

Anne Hathaway's Cottage

Design J2

Colours used:—

Clark's Anchor Stranded Cotton.

Pale Yellow F441, Gold F797, Light Orange F513, Rust F430, Shell Pink F501, Shaded Pink F884, Shaded Old-Rose F887, Light Red F596, Dark Red F599, Light Violet F412, Clematis F755, Shaded Blue F893, Pale Peacock Blue F482, Pale Green F573, Pale Spring Green F461, Spring Green F463, Light Bottle Green F408, Bronze Green F786, Light Grey F417, Mastic F244, Brown F834, Nigger F836, Pale Cream F601, White F721.

Abbreviations.—St.—stitch. Sd.—strands used in needle. Letters mentioned refer to the chart on this leaflet.

INSTRUCTIONS.

COTTAGE.

Walls. Shade in vertical long and short (2 sd.) st. F417, F601.

Timber. Work diagonally in long and short st., using at same time in needle 2 strands each F836, F834.

Door. St. as walls, F834, F244.

Bricks. (Under bow window, on left of right-hand upstairs window and chimney), 1 sd. F244 with 2 sd. F834 in needle together; work in straight sts. as traced.

Windows. Work as st. diagram No. 11, using F482 (2 sd.) with lattice F836 (1 sd.). Frame and curtains in stem st. (3 sd.) F721. Interior shadows, vertical long and short st. (2 sd.) F836, F244. Tiled roof to bow window, as bricks, plus F797.

Roof. Long and short st. (3 sd.) F834, F786, F244, then use two shades together in needle as follows: 2 sd. F797 with 1 sd. F244; 2 sd. F461 with 1 sd. F834, 2 sd. F797 with 1 sd. F430; 2 sd. F786 with 1 sd,

Full Size Detail of Worked Picture

INSTRUCTIONS—Continued from Page One

F244; shading under roof edge straight sts. (3 sd.) as traced, F836, F430 and F834 with F240. Finish edges with stem st. F836, F834.

Steps. Railings in diagonal satin st. (3 sd.) F721; steps horizontal long and short st. (2 sd.) F721, F417 with spaces between filled vertical satin st. F244. Outline whole with stem st. (1 sd.) F836.

Path. Long and short st. (2 sd.) F417, F601, F441 with stem st. outlines F244, F834.

Trees in Background. Straight st. and open lazy daisy st. (3 sd.) as traced using F408, F786, F461 also the following shades used together in needle 2 strands of the first named with one of the second: F408 with F786, F573 with F463; F441 with F461; F408 with F573; F786 with F573; F463 with F461. Branches in stem st. (3 sd.) F834, F244.

Foreground of Flowers, etc. (see chart).

A. Bushes. French knots F408 (3 sd.) then use together in needle 2 sd. F573 with 1 sd. F408, 2 sd. F463 with 1 sd. F573. Doves in front in satin st. (3 sd.) F721.

B. Bushes. As A using 2 sd. each in needle together, F408 with F834; F786 with F834, F463 with F244.

C. Bushes. As B using F834 with F786, F461 with F786, F461 with F244, F408 with F834, also F786 and F463 alone.

For flowers **D to J** use 3 sd.

D. Roses. French knots F834. Lazy daisy st. Leaves F573, F463.

E. White Flowers. French knots F721. Lazy daisy leaves F573.

F. Daisies. Straight st. F797, F441; french knot centres F836.

G. Hollyhock. Lazy daisy st. F513, centres F430, leaves F408.

H. Lupins. French knots F441.

J. Lupins. As H, F893.

K. Rambler Roses (4 sd.). French knots F884; lazy daisy leaves F461, F463.

For flowers **L to Z** use 6 sd. for flower heads, 4 sd. for centres and leaves, and 3 sd. for stems.

L. Delphiniums. French knots F893; lazy daisy leaves F463, F408; straight st. stems F834.

M. Roses. Raised rose st. F887, lazy daisy leaves F461, F463, F786; stems F408.

N. Pink Daisies. Lazy daisy st. F884; french knot centres F599; stems F573.

O. Daisies. Straight st. F441, F513; french knot centres F430; stems F573, F408.

P. Poppies. Satin st. F599, F596; leaves and stems F461, F463, F786.

Q. Californian Poppies. Satin st., F513, F430; leaves and stems F461, F463, F408.

R. Wallflowers. French knots, F599, F596, leaves and stems F461, F463, F786.

S. Blue Flowers. French knots F893.

T. Lavender. French knots F755, F412; stems F573, F408.

U. Roses. Raised rose st. F599, F596; leaves F463.

V. Daisies. Lazy daisy st. F441, F513; french knot centres F430; stems F408.

W. Daisies. Straight st., F887; french knot centres F721; stems F408.

X. Roses. Straight st. F441, F513 worked round a centre french knot F887; foliage F573, F463, F461, F786.

Y. Daisies. Lazy daisy st. F721; french knot centres F513, F834; leaves F786; stems F408.

Z. Canterbury Bells. Lazy daisy st. F755, F412; french knot centres F797; leaves and stems F573, F408.

AN EMBROIDERY FRAME

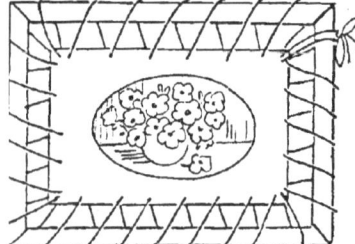

For the best results it is advisable to use an embroidery frame for this type of needlework. A small tambour or hoop frame will be found quite satisfactory, but if you cannot obtain one improvise a square frame as follows: Lay four narrow pieces of wood in position to form a square and nail at the corners. Place the article to be embroidered in the centre of the frame and lace the edges to the wood with string or strong cotton as shown in diagram.

If the article is larger than the frame, fold in the edges to fit.

Published by Wm. Briggs & Co., Ltd., Manchester 4.   Printed by Palatine Press, Manchester, 3.

100: Cut-work cloth made at Lenham Sanitorium, Kent 1948

have survived. Over a million packs of crests from Briggs were made up with the help of the Embroiderers' Guild. A touching story about one of them appeared in the *Daily Telegraph*, September 1940, 'Grenadier Guardsman Arthur Frost had started his embroidery in France during the previous winter and, while waiting on the beach during the evacuation of Dunkirk, he took the work from its pack and carried on with his stitching. Eventually he walked waist-deep into the sea, managed to get a boat and returned to England'. The embroidery was later finished and displayed.

Each pattern was made in a full range of articles but limited stocks could rarely guarantee making a matching set. Unfortunately, some service men and women were given more embroidery than they either wanted or had the time to finish and many half-embroidered table cloths are still languishing in homes today.

A short history of Briggs written in 1951 included a reference to an occupational therapy department; it is not known when it closed.

THE CRINOLINE LADY

This study of Art Needlework has tried to emphasise the best transfer designs but say the word 'transfer' and someone is sure to add 'crinoline lady'. From her arrival in the early 1900s she has been the most enduring and popular subject for embroidery. In spite of all the criticisms and thousands of variations which have been worked on every kind of household linen and clothing she is still with us. In 1956 the *Daily Telegraph* optimistically reported, 'Mr Colin Martin of Glasgow, Director of the Needlework Development Scheme, has finally killed off the crinoline lady who for years has decorated tea cosies and cushion covers. Leading transfer makers will soon be influenced by the new trends', but within a few days a letter was published, '..... the crinoline lady is a general favourite in sympathy with today's dress styles'. A 1995 catalogue of transfers, issued by Copelands Irish Linens and manufactured by Briggs, had twenty-eight ladies of dubious artistic merit.

The popularity of the crinoline lady coincided with the growth of middle class suburbs and accelerated at a phenomenal pace during the 1920s and 1930s. Many homes attempted a cottage style with gables, half-timbering and decorative brickwork. Their owners planted what they considered a cottage garden with pristine lawns and borders overflowing with old fashioned flowers - hollyhocks, lupins, lavender and daisies, trellis work and arches heavy with rambling roses over a crazy paved path leading to a pool or sundial - the perfect setting for a crinoline lady (*fig 101*).

Unfortunately, the clothes worn by crinoline ladies were rarely historically accurate. Although the artists could have referred to books on costume or examples in museums they seem to have relied heavily on their imaginations and drew figures in a hotchpotch of styles. Even if a dress was drawn correctly, the chances of the almost obligatory hat belonging to the same period were slim; a face was difficult to embroider so the best solution was to obscure it with a large bonnet. Some dresses were vaguely eighteenth century 'Gainsborough girls', other depicted ladies tending their garden in a Victorian ballgown. One transfer suitable for a tea cosy was inspired by 'Tchaikovsky's Valse with a dainty figure amid bouquets of flowers'. Even magazines published for the wives of successful middle-class businessmen had crinoline ladies; *Good Housekeeping*, 1926, had a particularly sentimental picture with a cross stitch motto:

> 'Two old friends with a cup of tea,
> One of them you, one of them me.'

Gentlemen were seldom shown but the favoured dress was silk coat and breeches, tricorn hat and powdered wig, often made easier to embroider by hiding most of him behind his lady's voluminous skirt.

It is impossible to date an embroidered crinoline lady, if a transfer sold well it was kept in production indefinitely or reissued at intervals over a long period. In the 1930s Briggs had catalogues devoted to this subject and employed one woman artist who believed she had a talent for it and drew nothing else. Every manufacturer produced them. Boynton & Turner put them on everything and believed the bigger the better, one colossal crinoline formed a complete apron with a parasol for the pocket, another idea used one to give the shape to each mat for a cheval set. Fairistytch suggested the use of appliqué. There were transfers sold with net to enhance the work and others suitable for embroidery or silver paper work. She was used for countless free gifts for diverse merchandise, even *Tobler* chocolate and *Reveille for the Weekend*.

The crinoline lady has had more adverse criticism than any other embroidery design, but whatever one's opinion she cannot be ignored. May be she is folk art - even the very collectable Clarice Cliff put one in her *Idyll* pattern.

101 Appliqué and surface stitchery worked in Madeira for catalogue Illustration Fairistytch 1940

It is worth noting that, 60's transfers were not all about crinoline ladies. Many other attractive designs were produced during this period, *(figs 102, 103)* but by now the popularity of the hot iron transfer had waned in favour of other types of embroidery.

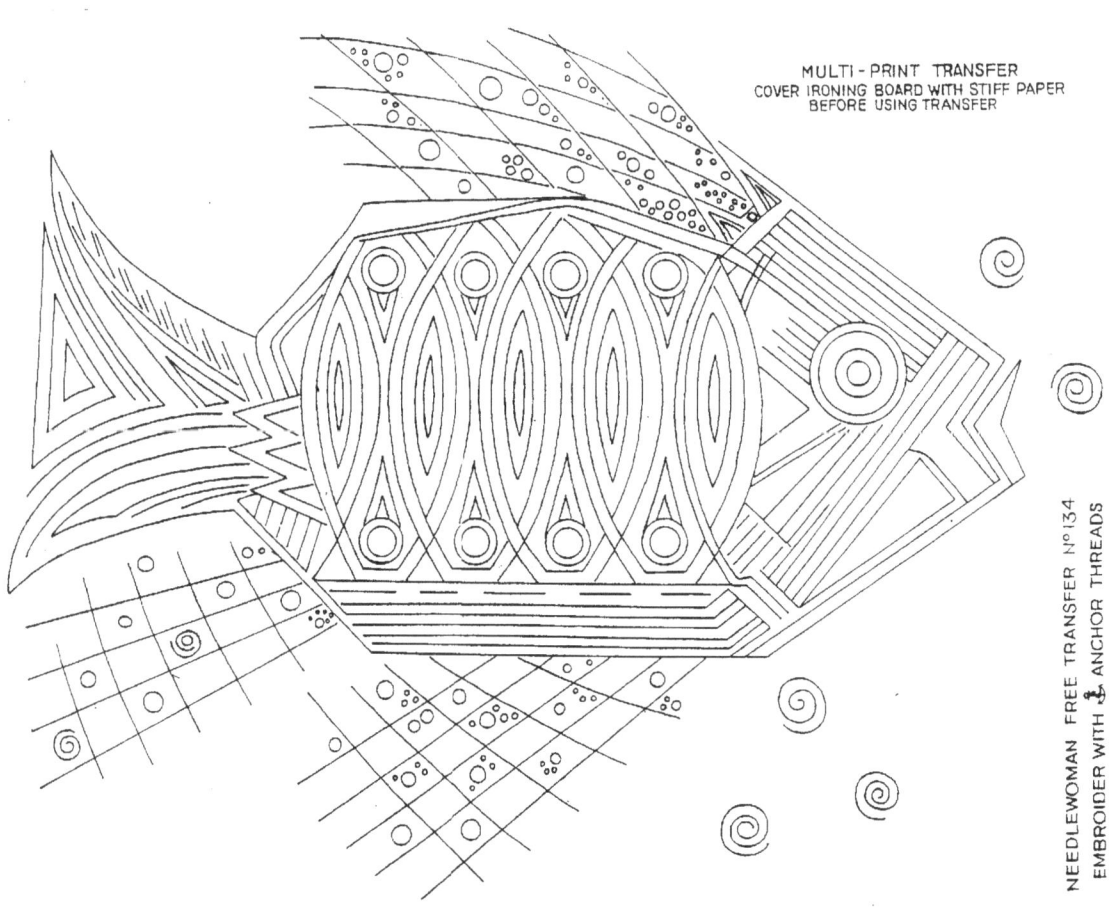

102: Design influenced by post-war art school students 1960s, but it did not affect the popularity of the crinoline lady

103: Design influenced by post-war Scandinavian embroidery. Briggs late 1960s-1970s

APPENDIX

BRIGGS NEEDLE ETCHINGS
available at various times between 1930-1960s

* also available tinted in sepia 1935-39 approximately

\+ available for occupational therapy 1939-45, not the home market until after the war

HISTORIC CASTLES
7½ x 10 inches, optional frame 12½ x 15 inches

+ Alnwick	+ Denbigh	+ Neidpath
+ Arundel	+ Dover	+ Newark
+ Appleby	Dublin	Newcastle-on-Tyne
+ Balmoral	+ Dunnottar	+ Nottingham
Barnard	+ Durham	Oystermouth
+ Beaumaris	+ Edinburgh	+ Palace of Holyrood House
Bishop Auckland (castle gate)	+ Glamis	+ Peel IOM
+ Bodiam	+ Goodrich	+ Pembroke
+ Bolton	Guildford	+ Richmond
+ Brechin	+ Harlech	Roch
Broughton Ferry	+ Hampton Court Palace	Rochester
+ Buckingham Palace	Haverfordwest	Rushen IOM
+ Caerlaverock	+ Huntly	Ruthin
Caernarvon	+ Herstmonceaux	+ Scarborough
+ Caerphilly	Inverness	+ Shrewsbury
Cardiff	+ Kenilworth	+ Stirling
+ Carew	+ Kingswear	Stirling (from back-walk)
+ Carlisle	+ Knaresborough	+ St Andrews
+ Carisbrooke	+ Lancaster	+ Stokesay
+ Chepstow	+ Loudoun	+ Warwick
Claypotts	+ Ludlow	+ Warkworth
+ Conway	+ McClellans	+ Windsor
Cornet	+ Mains, Dundee	
+ Criccieth	+ Manorbier	

CATHEDRALS and CHURCHES
7½ x 10 inches, optional frame 12½ x 15 inches

	Armagh, St Patrick's Protestant	Grantham	+	Peterborough
	Armagh, St Patrick's RC	Great Hampden		Quarrington
+	Belfast	Haddington, Church of	+	Ripon
	Beverley St Mary's	St Mary		Rotherham, All Saints
	Bishop Auckland	Halifax	+	Salisbury
+	Boston, St Botolph's (SE view)	Hartlepool, St Hilda's		Shaftesbury, St Peter's
	Boston, St Botolph's (NW view)	+ Hereford	+	Sheffield
	Brechin	Hexham		Sleaford
+	Bristol	Hull, Holy Trinity		Stafford, St Mary's
	Bristol, from the South	+ Inverness		Stockport, Church of Our
+	Canterbury	Kingston-upon-Hull,		Lady & Apostles
+	Carlisle	St Mary's		St Andrew's
+	Chester	Kirk Braddon		St Andrew's, Blackfriars
+	Chesterfield, crooked spire	Lancaster		ruins
	Chorley St Peter's	Leeds		St Andrew's, Kirkella
+	Chichester	Leeds, St Adrian's	+	St Asaph's
	Christchurch	Leicester, Holy Trinity	+	St Columb's, Londonderry
	Cromer	+ Lichfield	+	St Giles', Edinburgh
+	Derby	Lichfield, St Chad's	+	St Machar's, Aberdeen
	Doncaster St George	+ Lincoln		St Machar's (Tower view)
	Dublin	+ Liverpool	+	St Magnus, Kirkwall
	Dundee Methodist	+ Liverpool Cathedral War	+	St Mary's, Redcliffe
+	Durham	Memorial		St Paul's, Dundee
	Durham, view from river	+ Liverpool Cathedral	+	St Paul's, London
	Edinburgh, Cathedral Church of	Choir		Taunton, St Mary's
	St Mary	+ Llandaff	+	Truro
+	Elgin	+ Louth		Tynemouth Priory
+	Ely	Maidstone, All Saints	+	Wakefield
+	Exeter	+ Manchester	+	Wells
	Fairfield	Minehead	+	Winchester
	Falkirk	Nantwich, St Mary's		Woodburn
	Frome, St John the Baptist	+ Newcastle	+	Worcester
	Gellygaer	+ Norwich		Worksop
+	Glasgow	Nottingham, St Barnabas		Wrexham
+	Gloucester	Osbournby		

ABBEYS and MINSTERS
7½ x 10 inches, optional frame 12½ x 15 inches

+	Arbroath	+	Kelso	+	St Alban's
+	Bath		Kelso (near view)	+	Sweetheart
+	Beverley	+	Kirkstall	+	Tewkesbury
+	Bolton	+	Lincluden		Tintern
+	Buckfast	+	Malvern Priory		Valle Crucis
	Bury St Edmund's		Melrose	+	Welbeck
	Dryburgh		Paisley		Westminster
+	Dundrenan	+	Pluscarden		Westminster (interior)
+	Dunfermaline	+	Rievaulx		Whitby
+	Fountains		Roman Bath	+	York Minster
+	Furness	+	Selby		York Minster (front view)
+	Jedburgh	+	Sherbourne		

COLLEGES and UNIVERSITIES
7½ x 10 inches, optional frame 12½ x 15 inches

Aberdeen, King's College (Tower)	Edinburgh, Daniel Stewart's College	Marishal (Tower & Chapel)
Aberdeen, King's College (full view)	Edinburgh, George Herist School	+ Merton College, Oxford
+ All Souls College, Oxford	+ Edinburgh, George Watson Ladies College	+ New College, Oxford
+ Balliol College, Oxford	+ Emmanuel College, Cambridge	+ Oriel College, Oxford
+ Bangor University	+ Exeter College, Oxford	Paisley, John Neilson School
+ Brasenose College, Oxford	Glasgow (distant view)	+ Pembroke College, Oxford
+ Bridge of Sighs, St John's	Glasgow (front view)	+ Queen's College, Cambridge
+ Bristol University	+ Glasgow University	Sherbourne, (the Quadrangle)
+ Caius College, Cambridge	Huntley	St Andrew's
+ Christ's College, Cambridge	+ Jesus College, Cambridge	+ St John's College, Cambridge
+ Corpus Christi College, Oxford	+ King's College, Cambridge	+ St John's College, Oxford
Dublin, Trinity	+ Magdalen College, Oxford	+ Tom Tower, Christchurch College
Edinburgh	+ Marischal (full view)	+ Trinity College, Cambridge
		+ University College, Oxford
		Wakefield Silacoates School

PLACES of LOCAL INTEREST
Most 7 x 10 inches, some smaller if not supplied with frame

Abbotsford	Dundee, Old Tower and Churches	Looe, Banjo Pier
Aberdeen The Market Cross		Looe, Old Guildhall
Alva Cochrane House	Dundee, Old Town House	Looe, The Harbour and Bridge
Alva House	Dundee, Royal Arch	Lynmouth, Mars Hill
+ Ann Hathaway's Cottage	Dunster High Street	Linton, North Walk
Ayr Seafield Hospital	East Grinstead, St Margaret's Convent	Manchester, The Shambles
Balmasharmer War Memorial		Montrose Suspension Bridge
	Edinburgh, Sir Walter Scott's Monument	Newcastle, Tyne Bridge
Banchory, Brig-o-Fench		Newtownards, Clandaboye Helen's Tower
Bathgate Academy	+ Elgin, St Giles' Church	
Bedord Boys Modern School	Exeter Guildhall	Newtownards, Scrabo
	Falkirk High Street	Newquay, The Harbour
Bedford School	Forfar, Reid Hall	Newquay, The Island
Belfast City Hall	Forth Bridge	+ Scottish War Memorial
Berwick Royal Border Bridge	Galashield's War Memorial	Selworthy, Green Cottages
	Glasgow Art Galleries	+ Shakespeare's Birthplace
Blackpool Stanley Park	Godalming, Charterhouse	Sheffield Town Hall
Brechin Bridge	Guildford Guildhall	Stirling, Wallace Monument
Buckie Craigmin Bridge	Hayes, Birthplace of Sir Walter Raleigh	St Andrew's, The Harbour
Burghley House		St Andrew's, North Street
Bury St Edmund's Norman Tower	Hereford Old House	St Andrew's, The Pends
	Inverness Castle and Suspension Bridge	St Andrew's, West Port
Buxton Crescent		St Michael's Mount
Canterbury Norman Staircase	Ipswich, Ancient House	Stratford-on-Avon, Swan Inn
	Jesmond Dene	Swansea Civic Centre
Canterbury, 'The Weavers'	Kirkcaldie War Memorial	Tipperary, Rock of Cashe and Ruins
Cardiff City Hall	Kirknall, The Earls' Palace	
Carmarthen Bridge	Lands End	Torpichen Quhain and Church
Chorley Astley Hall	Laurencekirk, Johnston's Tower	Tunbridge Wells, The Pantiles
+ Clovelly High Street		Wakefield, The Chantry
Cockington Forge	Leeds Town Hall	Whitley Bay, St Mary's Lighthouse
Clifton Suspension Bridge	Linlithgow Palace	
Crail Town Hall	+ Liverpool, St George's Hall	Worksop, Clumber House
Crieff 'Sma Glen'	Llandrindod Wells, Lake and Chalet	Worksop, Thoresby Hall
Cromer Hall		
Cromer Promenade	Llandrindod Wells, Rock Spa	and others
David Livingstone's Birthplace	Llandudno, Happy Valley	
	Llangollen, Plas Newydd	
Dundee, Caird Hall	Londonderry Town Hall	

FAMOUS OLD INNS
8 x 5½ inches mounted on frames 12½ x 10 inches

*	Alfriston	The Star	*	Ludlow	The Angel
	Broadway	The Lygon Arms		Ludlow	The Feathers
*	Canterbury	The Falstaff		Norton St Philip	The George
	Chiswell	The King's Head		Oxford	Golden Cross
*	Cobham	The Leather Bottle		Rowsley	The Peacock
	Coxwold	The Falkenbery Arms		Rye	The Mermaid
	Coxwold	Shandy Hall	*	St Albans	The Fighting Cocks
*	Gloucester	The New Inn	*	Shrewsbury	King's Head
	Hatfield	The Eight Bells		Stratford-on-Avon	The Garrick
	Henley	The Bell	*	Tonbridge	The Chequers
*	Higham	The Dolphin		Wakefield	Six Chimneys
	Hinton Admiral	Cat and Fiddle	*	Weobley	The Red Lion
	Hurley	The Bell	*	West Looe	The Jolly Sailor
*	London	Staple's Inn		Winchester	Hostel of God Begot
	Long Wittenham	The Barley Mow		plus possible others	

COUNTY MAPS 1930s
11½ x 9 inches mounted on plywood frames 12½ x 15 inches.
All the counties in the British Isles with border lines tinted by hand.

CHINESE PICTURES No Titles
7¼ x 11 inches on wooden frame 12½ x 15 inches.
Two scenes inspired by the Chinese Art Exhibition c1935.

FAMOUS OLD SHIPS c1950
7½ x 10 inches on frames 12½ x 15 inches.

+ Cutty Sark	+ Great Harry	+ Victory	+ Golden Hind	+ Mayflower

Additionally at 5¾ x 3½ inches - two etchings of ships 'Sea Shanty'

LONDON VIEWS
Less than 7 x 10 inches, not supplied with frame.

+ Tower Bridge	+ Mansion House	Eros Statue
+ Old Curiosity Shop	+ Houses of Parliament	Tower of London

RURAL SCENES No lettering

5¾ x 4¼ inches	Two horses ploughing in rural landscape Horse and haycart with thatched cottage Haymaking
6 x 8 inches	Thatched cottage and stone wall Tiled cottage, stone wall, steps and trees Tiled cottage with sea view Timber-framed cottage and another cottage Timber-framed cottage and road over bridge Thatched cottage with stone bridge Stage coach Lady and man skating Huntsman and dog Fishing boat on the beach

DOGS 1950
8 x 11 inches

Airedale terrier	Chow Chow	Sealyham Terrier
Alsatian	English Setter	Scottish Terrier
Borzoi	Old English Sheep Dog	Spaniel
Bulldog	Pekinese	Wire-Haired Fox Terrier
Cairn	Pug	possibly others

REGIMENTAL and OTHER BADGES

Army Air Corps	King's Own Scottish Light Infantry	Royal Engineers
Army Air Corps (Glider Pilot)		Royal Fusiliers
Army Badge	King's Regiment	Royal Horse Guards
Army Catering Corps	King's Royal Rifle Corps	Royal Inniskillen Fusiliers
Army Dental Corps	King's Shropshire Light Infantry	Royal Irish Fusiliers
Army Educational Corps	Lancashire Fusiliers	Royal Marines
Army Physical Training Corps	Land Army	Royal Navy
Army Training Corps	Leicestershire Regiment	Royal Norfolk Regiment
Argyll & Sutherland Highlanders	Life Guards	Royal Northumberland Fusiliers
Auxiliary Military Pioneer Corps	Lincolnshire Regiment	
Auxiliary Territorial Service	London Scottish	Royal Scots
Bedfordshire & Hertfordshire Regiment	Lowland Regiment	Royal Scots Fusiliers
	Loyal Regiment	Royal Sussex Regiment
Black Watch	Manchester Regiment	Royal Warwickshire Regiment
Border Regiment	Merchant Navy	Royal Welsh Regiment
Buffs	Merchant Navy Officer's Standard Badge	Scots Greys
Cameron Highlanders		Scots Guards
Cameronians	Middlesex Regiment	Seaforth Highlanders
Canadian Forces	Military Police	Somerset Light Infantry
Canadian National Emblem	Monmouthshire Regiment	South Lancashire Regiment
Cheshire Regiment	National Fire Service	South Staffordshire Regiment
Coldstream Guards	Northamptonshire Regiment	Territorial Army Nursing Service
Corporation of Trinity House	North Staffordshire Regiment	
Devonshire Regiment	Oxfordshire & Buckinghamshire Light Infantry	Welsh Guards
Dorsetshire Regiment		Welsh Regiment
Duke of Cornwall's Light Infantry	Parachute Regiment	West Yorkshire Regiment
Duke of Wellington's Regiment (West Riding)	Queen Alexandra's Imperial Military Nursing Service	Wiltshire Regiment
		Women's Royal Naval Service
Durham Light Infantry	Queen's Bays	Worcestershire Regiment
East Surrey Regiment	Queen's Own Royal West Kent Regiment	York & Lancaster Regiment
East Lancashire Regiment		1st King's Dragoon Guards
East Yorkshire Regiment	Queen's Royal Regiment	3rd Carabiniers
Essex Regiment	Reconaissance Corps	3rd King's Own Hussars
Fleet Air Arm	Rifle Brigade	4th Queen's Own Hussars
Green Howards	Royal Air Force	4th/7th Royal Dragoon Guards
Gloucestershire Regiment	Royal Armoured Corps	5th Inniskillen Dragoon Guards
Gordon Highlanders	Royal Army Chaplain's Department	7th Queen's Own Hussars
Grenadier Guards		8th King's Royal Irish Hussars
Hampshire Regiment	Royal Army Medical Corps	9th Queen's Royal Lancers
Highland Light Infantry	Royal Army Ordnance Corps	10th Royal Hussars
Highland Regiment	Royal Army Pay Corps	11th Hussars
Honorable Artillery Company	Royal Army Service Corps	12th Royal Lancers
Intelligence Corps	Royal Army Veterinary Corps	13th/18th Royal Hussars
Irish Guards	Royal Berkshire Regiment	14th/20th King's Hussars
King's Own Royal Regiment	Royal Corps of Signals	15th/19th King's Royal Hussars
King's Own Scottish Borderers	Royal Dragoons	
	Royal Electrical & Mechanical Engineers	16th/5th Lancers
		17th/21st Lancers

SOURCES OF ART NEEDLEWORK DESIGNS
Used for this book

Ladies Magazines

Everywoman
Fancy Needlework
Fashions for All
Femme chez Elle
Good Housekeeping
Good Needlework
Good Needlework and Knitting
Hamsworth's Magazine
Hers
Home Chat
Homes and Gardens
Housewife
Lady's World
Leaches Knitting and Handicraft
Mademoiselle
Miss Modern
Modern Home
Modern Woman
My Home

Needle and Thread
Needlecraft Monthly
Needlework Illustrated
Needlewoman and Needlecraft
People's Friend
Pins and Needles
Stitchcraft
The Needlewoman
Weldon's Bazaar of Children's Fashions
Weldon's Ladies Journal
Woman
Woman's Day
Woman's Friend
Woman's Own
Woman's Pictorial
Woman's Realm
Woman's Weekly
Woman's World
etc

Others

Bestway Dress Patterns
Butterick Fashion Guide
Daily Herald
Daily Telegraph
Fleetway Amalgamated Press
McCalls dress patterns
Reveille
Schoolmistress

Simplicity Dress Patterns
Sunday Chronicle
Sunday Graphic
Sunday Stories
Teacher's World
Tobler Chocolate
William Hollins with Vyella
etc

BIBLIOGRAPHY

There are no books with details about hot-iron transfers, they receive no more than a mention anywhere. However, books concerned with all aspects of art during the period are interesting and the following have been particularly useful:

Book	Author	Publisher
Arts and Crafts Style	Isabelle Anscombe	Phaidon
Art Nouveau	Mario Amaya	Schocken Books, New York
A Guide to Art Nouveau Style	William Hardy	Grange Books
Modern Decorative Art	M & R Adams	Batsford
Modern Decorative Art in England	W G Paulson Townsend	Batsford
The Decorative Twenties	Martin Battersby	Studio Vista
The Decorative Thirties	Martin Battersby	Studio Vista
C20th Embroidery in Great Britain	Constance Howard	Batsford

INDEX

Alphabets, 13, 16, 18, 21
Anchor stranded cotton, 79
Ann Macbeth, 34, 36, 71
Art Deco, 3, 28, 33, 47, 48, 49, 53, 55
Art Needlework, 3, 4, 5, 18, 21, 23, 24, 28, 29, 34, 36, 37, 41, 43, 48, 63, 66, 71, 72, 79, 84
Art Nouveau, 3, 20, 34, 36, 37, 41, 96
Arthur Mackmurdo, 20
Arts and Crafts Movement, 4
Australia, 28, 72
Beckett, 2, 24, 25, 27, 28, 29
Berlin wool-work, 4, 5, 13, 16, 17, 48
Blanche Fitzmaurice Portfolio of Artistic Needlework, 19, 20, 36
Boynton & Turner, 29, 85
Boynton & Turner Transfers, 29
Braid lace, 39
Braiding, 13, 14, 15, 17
Briggs, 2, 3, 6, 7, 9, 10, 12, 13, 14, 15, 16, 17, 18, 19, 21, 22, 24, 25, 26, 28, 29, 31, 36, 39, 42, 51, 52, 57, 58, 59, 61, 62, 63, 64, 66, 68, 72, 74, 76, 78, 79, 83, 84
Canada, 72
Celtic, 17, 34
Century Guild, 20
City of London Trade School, 28
Clarice Cliff, 85
Coats Group, 6, 28, 29, 42
Commenced (work), 12, 23, 24, 34, 48, 57
Constance Brown, 20
Constance Howard, 53, 71, 96
Copelands, 17, 84
Crewel Work, 15, 17, 31
Crinoline lady, 63, 84, 85
Daily Telegraph, 4, 78, 83, 84, 95
Deighton Brothers, 9
Deighton's, 4, 6, 7, 12, 17, 18, 24, 25, 28, 29, 34, 36, 39, 41, 48, 57, 61, 64, 66, 72, 76, 79

Dublin, 9, 74, 88, 89, 90
Ecclesiastical, 13, 17, 23, 68, 89, 91
Edward Burne-Jones, 19, 34
Embroiderers Guild, 47, 48
Embroidery, 4, 5, 6, 13, 16, 17, 19, 20, 21, 23, 24, 25, 28, 29, 31, 41, 42, 47, 48, 49, 52, 53, 55, 58, 62, 63, 64, 68, 71, 76, 78, 79, 83, 84, 85, 96
English Sewing Cotton Co Ltd, 36, 41
Fairistytch, 2, 24, 26, 28, 29, 64, 85
Free transfer, 42, 43, 72
Glasgow School of Art, 24, 25, 27, 28, 34, 36, 39, 71, 84, 89, 90, 91
Gothic designs, 17
Harrods, 21, 28
Japanese, 16, 20
Joyce Grenfell, 78
Kate Greenaway, 16
Knox Linen Thread Company, 36
Lewis Day, 34
Liberty, 34, 36, 64
Madeira, 24, 25
Manchester School of Needlework, 41, 42
Massachusetts, 18
Miniature, 64, 66, 68
Mrs Archibald (Grace) Christie, 23, 24
Needle Etchings, 57, 59, 61, 79
New York, 17, 22, 96
New Zealand, 28
Northern Ireland, 9, 17, 31, 89, 91
Occupational therapy, 2, 58, 71, 78, 79, 83, 88
Old Bleach Linen Company, 31, 33, 49
Painting, 41, 61, 62, 71
Paper transfers, 12
Patent, 6, 9, 10, 12, 13
Pearsall, 23, 24, 49, 51
Penelope, 21, 22
Perforating, 6, 7, 8, 12, 26, 27
Public Record Office, 24

Ready traced, 13, 61
René Mackintosh, 36, 41
Royal College of Art, 20
Royal School of Art Needlework, 4, 19, 23, 29, 34, 37, 48, 72
Servicemen, 9, 19, 22, 29, 61, 71, 72, 74, 75, 76, 79, 94
Smocking, 17, 34
South Africa, 28
Sylko, 37
The Manchester School of Needlework, 21

Townswomen's Guild, 42
Traced linens, 22, 24, 28, 29, 31, 33, 76
United States of America, 9, 17, 18, 19, 22, 96
Victoria and Albert Museum, 48, 64
Victorian, 3, 5, 16, 37, 39, 47, 84
Walter Crane, 34
Weldon, 16, 17, 18, 22, 41, 42, 72, 95
William Deighton, 6, 8, 9, 12, 34
William Morris, 4, 34